TREASURY OF FRONTIER RELICS

Also by Les Beitz

Overlooked Treasures

TREASURY OF FRONTIER RELICS

A COLLECTOR'S GUIDE

SECOND EDITION, REVISED

BY

LES BEITZ

South Brunswick and New York: A. S. Barnes and Company
London: Thomas Yoseloff Ltd

© 1966 by Lester Beitz
© 1977 by A. S. Barnes and Co., Inc.
Library of Congress Catalogue Card Number: 75-20587

A. S. Barnes and Co., Inc.
Cranbury, New Jersey 08512

Thomas Yoseloff Ltd
Magdalen House
136–148 Tooley Street
London SE1 2TT, England

ISBN 0-498-01688-9
Printed in the United States of America

DEDICATED TO PAT WAGNER

who, after watching me rope
a critter or two, turned to
the range boss and said,
"He'll make a hand."

CONTENTS

FOREWORD

ALL OF MY LIFE I've had a natural bent to go poking around old ranch houses and cow pens and places like that, just to see what I might find.

Generally speaking, what I come across doesn't amount to a hill of beans, being nothing more unusual than a worn-out mule shoe or a rusty cinch ring. On the other hand, now and then I turn up some article odd enough to make me take a second look and maybe say to myself: "Gosh dog! Now that's a real curiosity, ain't it?" After which I generally tote it off home and pitch it onto the heap of similar junk that for years I've been piling up in the weeds outside my yard fence.

Well, I never had attached any real importance to this packrat habit of mine until sometime back when Les Beitz showed up at my place out here on the Llano River and got to digging around in my junk heap.

I read his book and learned that Les likely knows more about the value of western gear and relics than nearly any man in the country. I learned that I'm not just a packrat, that I'm a genuine collector of Western Americana! Most important, I learned that the stuff I've been piling up outside my yard fence is more like a treasure than a junk heap. Some will sell for actual cash!

If you've got a natural packrat bent, I'd advise you to get this book and use it to check through your collection. You never can tell what some of it may be worth.

FRED GIPSON

Mason, Texas

9

ACKNOWLEDGEMENTS

THIS IS MY first book. Making my way from front cover to back cover was pretty much like driving an old wagon across the prairie. Every now and then it would bog down hub deep or bust an axle, but there was always somebody around who would get behind the old rig and help me push it back on the trail. A couple of right fine smithies along the way helped me fix the busted axles, too. Without the help of all those fine folks, I just plumb couldn't have made the trip.

With sincere gratitude, I cite them here.

Joe A. Small, Publisher of *True West*, *Frontier Times* and *Old West* magazines, Austin, Texas.

Herschel C. Logan, Artist, Collector, Santa Ana, California.

Ralph A. Coffeen, Russell, Kansas.

Betty L. Elliott, Mountain View, California.

Robert Small, Austin, Texas.

Charles M. Waller, Salina, Kansas.

Jug and Mag Wayman, Indianapolis, Indiana.

And Cathie Wilson. Cathie was the compass that guided me along the trail. Without her, I'd probably still have the old wagon wedged between a couple of boulders way down in some ravine.

INTRODUCTION

FOUR OR FIVE years ago I ran into a goofy situation trying to buy an old branding iron. The codger in the junk shop hemmed and hawed around and finally said, "I don't know what it's worth—an' nobody else does, either, I reckon. How much ya' willin' to pay fer it?"

This put the monkey on my back. I said, "Two bucks," and he said, "Two an' a half." I bought the brand. Maybe he made a 400% profit on that iron—I didn't know. But I did know that if I were to continue developing my collection of Frontier Americana, I'd surely have to find out more about the stuff. It seemed to me that somewhere, someplace, there ought to be something to shed a little light on this situation, but there just wasn't much of anything in the way of collectors' reference that I could find.

To enable a feller to bargain with some degree of knowledge and understanding concerning the significance and worth of such items has motivated the preparation of this book. And I went about it this way.

In every junk shop, at every auction, in secondhand stores, and in all the other places where objects associated with the Old West were likely to appear, I carefully noted the number of them, area in which located, and prices asked with respect to condition. In effect, I amassed a passel of data and jottings that provided something of a fix as to how much these unclassified fragments of the old frontier ought to bring in relation to their actual prevalence or scarcity. This was purely statistical, of course, and didn't take into account all the priceless ingredients that go into this obsession called collecting. But it was a start.

I found, for instance, that in some sixty-odd shops or areas of possibility, not one chuck wagon box showed up. In Nebraska, of six junk shops explored, not a single brand iron appeared; however, in Texas, three similar shops produced a total of thirty-one old brands. But—and this is significant—of these thirty-one stamp irons, twenty-five were of Mexican origin. American cattle spreads were represented by the remaining six.

In a nutshell, the area of search and what was transpiring in that area of search seventy-five or a hundred years ago, will regulate what you will find and what you will pay for it. This is a distinct, specialized, completely different branch of collecting—a total departure from the field of General Americana. A collector in Ipswich, Massachusetts, may claim branding irons aren't nearly as common as I say they are because he can't find any. I fully expect also to have some feller tell me he has a Sharps buffalo rifle that his great-grandpappy used which he values at $2,000 and that my pricing of that fine weapon is ridiculous. I will have to leave it to the collector to decide whether or not he can afford sentiment.

Somebody had to kick this thing off, because the lore

of the old frontier demands it. The relics associated with the great American West warrant a place of their own and that's what I've attempted to give them. With the exception of those articles preserved in museums, or treasured in private homes, these unique and fascinating objects we call "Frontier Americana" are at present subjected to the harshest treatment Nature can hand out. They lie in fields, hang on the walls of leaky barns, mold in deserted prairie cellars, or rust in the shade of a *bois d'arc* pasture fence.

There are probably a thousand and one articles of western ancestry that are equally as deserving of mention as the ones covered here, but to do justice to the entire realm would necessitate another thousand and one pages. My primary intent is to relate a few facts and present a few examples of some typically representative items that were analogous to pioneer life and times—you might say, to bring up the "dawn" of these old treasures' day in the sun.

TREASURY OF FRONTIER RELICS

AT THE ROUNDUP CAMP

1. This remarkable picture was painted in 1904 at Cottonwood Camp, Colorado, by a 22-year-old artist named N. C. Wyeth. It depicts the very essence of the roundup camp, shortly after the range cook had shouted, "Come and get it!" Note the Bull Durham tag, three-tined fork, the polka dot bandanna, the Army issue cups, the striped vest, the leather cuffs, and the unusual proportions of the grub box. This is masterful western art. Works by Wyeth rank with those of Remington and Russell; a good bit more about this distinguished western illustrator appears in the chapter, "At The Golden Nugget."

GRUB BOX

Of ALL THE gear, accessories, objects and sundry paraphernalia that may be appropriately identified with western rangeland, nothing is so singularly distinctive as the chuck wagon mess box. This remark calls for some sort of qualification so let me put it this way. A Dutch oven or a Winchester .66 "Yellow Boy" could very well have been bought and used by a gent in Franklin County, North Carolina—but not so with the grub box. This is one little creation of the cattle country that simply was, is and shall remain a unique wooden affair that spells out just one term—ROUNDUP.

Like so many other things that were hand-fashioned for ranch use, no two are exactly alike. They all exemplified an elementary design, however, which rendered them perfectly suitable to the purpose for which they were intended. Essentially, this consisted of nothing more than a good-sized box or case with a hinged side, fitted with interior shelving or compartments. The box was fastened to the rear end of the ranch wagon, frequently an ordinary lumber wagon, by means of a clamp device or bolt arrangement to hold it to the wagon box planking. When the hinged side was let down and propped, it formed the cook's work table.

Some of these grub boxes are mighty fine examples of cabinetmaking with dovetail joinery, top notch tinsmithery in the special flour bin compartment, and finished off with elegant little porcelain drawer pulls. But most of them were of simple, sturdy construction pretty much devoid of ornamentation. I've seen some, rather squat, with a very acute slope to the hinged let-down door—others quite tall and gently sloped. Some are of shallow depth while others are proportioned so deep as to resemble a steamer trunk. However, they were all built to serve as portable storage cabinets with a cook-table lid and it is this feature that characterizes them from all other forms of cooking apparatus.

The grub box I have is a bodacious nice one. Swapped an old Waterbury shelf clock for it and feel that I came out best on the transaction because these old grub boxes simply aren't floating around like the mass-produced shelf or mantel clocks are. And I was extremely fortunate in securing all the "reloading tools" and mess gear with which the box was originally equipped. This included a couple of dough mixing pans, an old flapjack flipper with the inscription "Rumford's Baking Powder" heavily embossed on the handle, tin plates, knives, forks, spoons, and the quaintest set of five japanned tin cannisters I'd ever seen. These were the containers for such staples as salt, sugar, baking powder, coffee (Arbuckle's XXX, more than likely), ginger and the like. Flour, spuds, beans, sides of bacon, the bulkier stuff, was usually carried in the wagon along with the bedrolls.

The feller I swapped with was real happy with the old Waterbury as he dearly loves to tinker with such things.

And as I had been probing around for over a year looking for a good grub box, we both came off as delighted as the Katzenjammer Kids on the deal. It wasn't but a week or so later that I came upon a right decent old hand-forged pothook which adds measurably to the overall completeness of my relic.

Now as to the age of these grub boxes. Well, when Charlie Goodnight and his drovers pushed their longhorn

fies as a desirable addition to a collection representing frontier life. I don't think a feller ought to be fussy to the extent of turning his nose up at a box that's say, fifty or sixty years old because not every ranch had one; they're just not what you'd call plentiful.

While some museum curators or historical society directors might not settle for less than a truly classic example, I feel that the average collector would do well to

2. My chuck wagon box. A rare and treasured find.

critters northward in 1866, a rather primitive grub box went along. That box may be historically ascribed as the great-granddaddy of all chuck boxes—the oldest one in the world, I reckon. However, age, or rather great age, should not be considered a principal criterion in determining the worth of a chuck wagon box. Any genuine grub box that saw use on a cattle drive or roundup quali-

latch on to one even though it may be of circa 1915 vintage. Grub boxes weren't peddled from door to door as were Waterbury shelf clocks, so the collector ought to be a mite more tolerant on this item than he would be, perhaps, in bargaining for an old bootjack or some cavalry hoss bits.

Aside from the display aspects of an old grub box, the

thing has a downright practical adaptability, too. When mounted atop a narrow table it can be used as a sort of secretary, the drop lid providing a writing surface. The compartments or shelves are ideal for storage of books and other collectable miscellany.

As to value, the collector or dealer will recognize, I'm sure, that some of these chuck wagon boxes are remarkably fine examples of the carpenter's craft while others are of the simplest construction, ofttimes crude to the point of being little more than a converted shipping case. So there has to be a good bit of flexibility in arriving at a price that would be anywhere realistic. If it's a rather sorry box, $15 or $20 is the most it ought to bring. But if it's a really neat job that lends itself well as an eye-pleasing display cabinet or secretary, then eighty to a hundred frogskins wouldn't be a ridiculous offer.

It's kind of like asking what a horse is worth. He might be a nag or a Kentucky thoroughbred, so each has to be judged on its own individual merits. Then, too, if the pans and plates and tin cups are still in it, this would call for some extra consideration. And if it has historical significance such as association with a famous cattle spread like the XIT or the Running W or a similarly colorful heritage, it surely rates special recognition and consequent higher value. In short, the span on this relic is anywhere from $10 to, perhaps, $60 but if somebody comes up with old Charlie Goodnight's original grub box, it'll probably take a king's ranson to change ownership. Be that as it may, the thrill of finding a tolerably nice chuck wagon box is certainly an important milestone on the journey in quest of Frontier Americana.

DUTCH OVEN

OLD-TIME RANGE cookery could boast an item of cookware that was an institution in itself—the cast iron Dutch oven. This is the tub-shaped pot that was used to cook just about everything a hungry range rider would hanker for. Son-of-a-gun stew, brown beans, sourdough biscuits—practically the entire range bill of fare evolved around this all-purpose piece of cooking equipment. In the care of a cook who really knew his onions, the Dutch oven would yield the most savory concoctions imaginable because the principle of the whole affair was to cook the grub in its own natural juices and the oven was specifically devised for that purpose.

The top of the lid was flanged up around the rim edge to provide for fencing in a pile of hot coals. With a glowing heat beneath and a heap of live coals on top, the chuck cooked evenly. All the flavors flitted around inside that wonderful pot and the aroma that drifted away from the campfire would tempt the most demanding epicure. Yep! The Dutch oven produced superb vittles and certainly rates high as a collector's item in recognition of its outstanding service to the toilers of the open range.

As in all skillets, pots and utensils of this sort, they came in various sizes. Most range cooks packed along a couple or three of varying capacity in order to bake, stew or fry at the same time. A four-, three- and two-gallon set makes for an interesting display grouping and if the collector can acquire a potrack and a few pothooks, he can just about reproduce the old range cook's prairie kitchen.

Depending upon size, old Dutch ovens are worth anywhere from $8 to $20. The fact that cooking with oldfashioned Dutch ovens is very much in vogue today causes these relics to disappear rapidly from secondhand shops and junkie sheds. So one may have to go just a trifle higher to secure a nice, sound, old one. In dickering for one, be sure to check closely to insure that the lid is the right kind. Nothing is more disappointing to a collector than to locate one of these fascinating old relics and to find that it has an offbeat substitute lid. In this particular case, the oven lid is an integral part of the whole scheme of things, so it's an important factor to consider when you spot one.

3. A Dutch oven. The flanged lid and well-raised base accommodated coals atop and below—the secret to superb range fare.

COFFEE POT

THERE'S SIMPLY no telling how miserable life would have been on the open range (or in any other part of the West, for that matter) had it not been for plenty of steaming, black coffee. During roundup, there was seldom a spell from dawn till dusk that the five-gallon coffee pot wasn't putting forth its aromatic brew for the refreshment and contentment of saddle-weary crews. Those old pots and their contents represent another "institution" in the lore of the frontier—a status of preeminence that is richly deserved.

There are two types to be encountered, both of similar shape and design but each made of different material. The more common one was of heavy gauge tin, or "tinned iron," as some makers termed it; the other of lighter gauge material with graniteware or agateware coating. The pot had a wide base with acutely sloping sides, the lid diameter being barely half of the base diameter. It was equipped with a stout bail for suspension from a pothook over the open fire. A high handle was fitted to the side opposing the spout which afforded means to tilt the pot forward when pouring without removing it from the pothook.

Of course, there are coffee pots of frontier heritage that are of lesser capacity than the big five-gallon one cited here. Smaller cattle spreads, smaller coffee pots, I suppose. But the collector can suit himself on size and select the one that best fits into the decorative scheme of his den or study. It might be well in bargaining for one to be certain that the old pot doesn't leak too badly because a rust-pitted bottom is murder to restore. Reason for this sound bottom requirement is because someday you may

4. Range coffee pot—five-gallon.

want to brew up a real roundup coffee for guests and also because the ladies have a habit of confiscating those old pots for planters.

So let's say $22 to $25 for a right nice one; if the graniteware surface is not too badly chipped, $18; and ten bucks for sound, smaller ones.

BRANDING IRON

A COLLECTION OF things western certainly wouldn't be complete without a couple of old branding irons; maybe a running iron, if a feller can find a genuine one; and, perhaps, a copper branding ring. There was quite a batch of metal devices used to mark range cattle and horses and the usage of those irons constitute a colorful and ofttimes violent chapter in frontier history. Seems as if there's something adventurous and dramatic about an old branding iron that endows it with a certain appeal to collectors. Perhaps it's because the iron is a sort of personal monogram, an owner's mark, a kind of coat of arms of the cattle kingdom. Anyway, they're a fascinating tool of the trade and they all possess a character that lives and breathes Old West.

It's really surprising, but there are still a good many old brand irons knocking about the cattle country—and I mean old ones. There are also a lot of irons of welded

5. A typical stamp iron. This one was originally fitted to a wooden handle but most were forged with additional length to provide for a complete metal grip bar.

construction—late things—which are of little or no appeal to the informed western collector. It's simply a matter of realizing that branding irons are still used today, to a limited degree, and these late irons do have a tendency to show up along with the older ones. So the collector will have to be somewhat discriminating in selection.

The most common type is called a stamp iron in which the brand mark is forged to the handle rod forming a complete tool all in one piece. With this device the critter could be branded in one simple operation. Some brand designs, particularly the Mexican marks, are a combination of ornate scrolls, letters, objects, curlicues, geometric patterns and odd abstractions that called for a good bit of craftsmanship on the part of the smithy who forged them. But most American ranchers favored brand designs of simple, uncluttered pattern. I can't rightfully say that an ultra-fancy brand design should be more desirable than the simple Turkey Track or Lazy S brands, but each to his own liking in this matter. It is a fact, though, that famous brands such as the Running W, Bar X, Hash Knife or Diamond A command a premium because of their renown and significance in the lore of the great cattle empires.

Right now is a good time to pick up a couple of these wonderful relics because the choicest ones are seldom priced over $12 to $18. When the true historical significance of many of these irons is realized, the prices will skyrocket. I've got three beauties—the Pothook, Half Circle V, and Y Down irons—that I picked up for a song. Each is an oldtimer, loaded with all the excitement and drama of a bygone range.

But it's not so easy to acquire a real, bona fide running iron. These are the simple, hooked-end irons that were used principally by rustlers in running any type of brand mark. They were pretty much like a stove poker—the culprit merely heated the iron and altered, wrote, or drew the brand mark on the critter in the same manner as he'd inscribe with any pencil-like instrument. So the

6. Another of young Wyeth's paintings. This is one of the very few works in western illustration showing the rustlers camp and the principal tool of their trade—the running iron.

rub here is to establish whether the iron is an actual running iron or whether it's a hooked rod intended for some other purpose. This is a mean task and about the only way one could be certain beyond a doubt that he has the real McCoy is to have some legal-looking "Exhibit A" documentation to support its authenticity. If some old sheriff or constable produces one from his confiscation department and furnishes absolute proof that it's a rip-roaring, real running iron, I'd be awful tempted to part with two twenty-dollar bills in exchange.

Brand rings are another device that can easily be of dubious origin. These were nothing more than copper hoops, much on the order of a kid's oversize teething ring, which was manipulated with stick handles to run any kind of brand. Their chief advantage was compactness as they could easily be tied to a saddle string, whereas the stamp irons were rather clumsy to tote on horseback. Brand rings were not employed to the extent of the other devices, however, and an authentic one falls into the same category as the running iron. The old constable would have to come up with a gilt-edged guarantee on this gadget, also, before I'd acknowledge it as true Frontier Americana.

HUB NUT WRENCH

SOME FOLKS USE wagon wrench, wheel wrench, axle wrench, hub wrench, and a half-dozen similarly descriptive names to identify this basic frontier tool. Can't say

7. *Hub nut wrench found in an abandoned wagon shed near old Fort Harker, Kansas.*

that I know of a specific term or manner in which they should be labeled, but every ranch wagon or farm rig had one. So call it what you will, they're a pretty important fragment of the Old West.

It might be appropriate to dwell here for a moment or two on this business of "fragmenta." Certain relics of early frontier life have assumed a lofty eminence, a kind of monumental stature. A good example is the Colt .45 or a Wells Fargo strong box. But it's a cinch that neither of these two significant antiques would have made the grade if it were not for hoss bits, muleshoes, axle grease and wagon wrenches. Can't say that a gob of axle grease makes an intriguing item for display but an old hub nut wrench does have a rugged, homely sort of eye-arresting appeal. Perhaps it seems extreme to relate objects in this manner but actually it was a goodly passel of those little accessories and "fragmenta" that played a key role in the development and expansion of the vast frontier. Because of their seeming insignificance, they've been relegated to the limbo of rural trash piles. To rescue one is to preserve a vital link to the West as it really was.

Well, there's nothing very decorative about a hub nut wrench; these implements can never hope to compete with old branding irons in their appeal to collectors. But I think every comprehensive collection of things western ought to contain one, if nothing more than a mute tribute to the wagon boss or ranch hand who might possibly have used it to plod on a little farther westward.

The one in my collection, of heavy iron bar stock, was forged by some smithy for use on a pretty good-sized wagon wheel. The jaw takes a two-inch nut; the grip handle is a little over ten inches long. They were made, of course, for every kind of wagon, coach, rig and vehicle so the sizes of these tools vary considerably. Saw one not so long ago with about a three-quarter inch jaw span, undoubtedly for use on a buckboard or similarly light rig.

Since this homely tool falls into the relatively unglamorous category referred to as "fragmenta," $4 or $5 wouldn't be out of line to pay for a typical one. This modest pricing has been influenced largely because wagons and wagon wrenches by the thousands were made and used from Maine to Florida as well as from St. Louis to San Francisco, so a western one will be no different from its eastern cousin. The chief consideration here is that the lowly nut wrench did figure with marked effect in the great panorama of western history. It deserves a small measure of acclaim.

TABLE OF VALUES

The column on the right denotes the degree of scarcity of each relic. The numbers assign a scarcity factor as follows: 1–3 common, 4–6 scarce, 7–9 rare.

Relic	Fair	Good	Excellent	Scarcity Factor
Branding Irons				
Brand Ring	$20	$30	$ 35–40	7
Running Iron	$22	$35	$ 40+	8
Stamp Iron	$ 8–10	$12–14	$ 15–18	5
Coffee Pots				
Agate or				
Graniteware	$10–12	$18	$ 25	3
Tinned Iron	$ 8–10	$15–18	$ 22–24	2
Dutch Ovens				
4-Gallon	$12	$18	$ 22	3
3-Gallon	$ 6	$ 9	$ 12	2
2-Gallon	$ 5	$ 8	$ 10	1
Grub Box	$20–25	$40–50	$100+	8
Hub-Nut Wrench	$ 2	$ 3.50	$ 5	1

AT THE BARN

8. *This dramatic painting of a frontier marshal and his posse is another superb work by the illustrator Wyeth. Done in 1907 when the artist was 25 years of age, it's much more than a story illustration; it's western art of the finest achievement.*

OX YOKE

YOKES BY WHICH draught oxen were controlled have been quite extensively collected as a form of primitive Americana. The graceful sweep of contour in the outline of the double yoke has strongly influenced their acceptance as attractive items of decoration. Usually mounted over a mantel or as the crest of an arch, they have gained favor largely because of interesting effect rather than through their historical attributes. For purposes here, however, the decorative qualities of old ox yokes will have to take a back seat with primary consideration afforded to their scarcity and value.

Although in pretty general use throughout the West for a hundred years and more, ox yokes are seldom found lying around old stables and wagon sheds these days. The double yoke, about four feet long with an up and over curve at each end, is somewhat more common than the single yoke. The characteristics of these two types are quite self-explanatory; the single yoke is merely one

9. *Well preserved ox yoke which was used in central Kansas in the 1880s.*

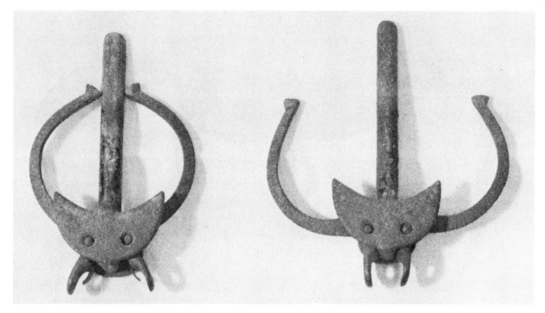

10. *Patented ox yoke pins used to hold the bows in place. Patented in the 1880s. Illustration shows the pins opened and closed. They were held in a closed position by a spring in the head.*

half of the double yoke with some little variation in the metal fittings or rigging apparatus.

The little metal keys with which the oxbows were wedged to keep from sliding out of the yoke are rather scarce. Seems as if little accessories like these are frequently astray from the parent relic. Reason for mention of such detail is that completeness is a most desirable asset in all phases of collecting and prices simply must be discounted if the piece has a missing component. Firearm collectors are exceptionally discriminating in insisting that the numbers on each part of an antique weapon be serially matched. Ox yoke keys and oxbows should be no exception and, if part and parcel of the original relic, warrant a premium.

It goes without saying that some ox yokes were made better than others, that some will require a replacement part or general reconditioning of sorts, and that occasionally one will be found in tip-top shape. But most of those old ox yokes saw mighty hard usage and that's why I've remarked pointedly on the premium and discount aspects which must be applied.

Go $60 to $75 for one that's in good shape, conditioning your offer to account for the quality of craftsmanship that was originally employed in the making of the piece. **Descend your valuation down to $15 or $20 if the relic has** bad splits, broken or missing oxbows, heavily rust-pitted iron fittings, lost keys, etc. Since the single yoke is a little more scarce than the standard double yoke, it's worth a ten percent premium, the above cited condition factors applicable, of course.

OXSHOES

THERE'S JUST not a whole lot that can be said about old oxshoes except that they're intensely interesting things;

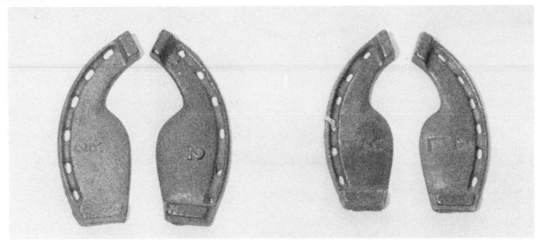

11. Old oxshoes.

they're significant in the story of westward emigrant trains and the expansion of the vast frontier; and that they're fittin' and proper to be displayed with old ox yokes and wagon gear—and that's about all a feller can say about them. But, in a way, that's a'plenty!

It is such lowly objects as these that deserve a special little niche in the cabinet of the western collector because an old oxshoe reflects, in a most dramatic way, the lore of the trail, those long, rough overland journeys that actually opened the door to a western empire. Well, oxen were shod with forged iron soles in South Carolina and Nova Scotia as well as by smithies at terminal points like St. Louis. So it's awfully hard to say that one possesses a true frontier heritage unless it has been recovered at a western site. Some collectors are real sticklers for such authenticity in its most exacting sense, but I think any old oxshoe ought to be considered worthy of inclusion in a grouping of relics that are representative of frontier life and times.

Certain old muleshoes and horseshoes belong in this same category. And old shoeing nails and smithy tongs—I could go on and on citing scores of wonderful things that reflect the excitement and color of those rip-roaring

days which could, and should, be permitted to have their say in the western panorama.

So, find an old muleshoe or oxshoe, if you can. I sometimes glance up at the homely old oxshoe I have and muse for a moment or two, envisioning the husky feller who fashioned it and the endless miles it has been trod with the hoof of the beast that bore it. It's a sad-looking **old hunk of iron but I like it. Probably worth two dollars or so—but the point here is that it's an intriguing symbol of the coarse, rugged, plodding and bold life of a Westerner. It tells me a great story and I wouldn't trade it for the best steak dinner in town.**

PACK SADDLE

THE ROCKY Mountain crosstree or sawbuck type pack saddle certainly warrants a couple square feet of floor space in a display of western relics. Old-time packers and their mule trains were the mainstay to many a frontier outpost and the gear of that trade is exceedingly difficult to locate these days.

Old cavalry and stockmen's saddles have had something of an extended life span because the era of the horse has not yet passed entirely from our midst. But the panniers and pack saddles are all about gone; the few that have survived might well be regarded as monumental to the ornery critters that bore them.

All these early pack saddles are quaint in their hand-fashioned joinery. They have a primitive, rustic charm that is accented by all the little irregularities about them. The wooden peg assembly of the X framing has a great deal of eye appeal and it's a shame that the rascally things are not adaptable to conversion into a functional or utilitarian furnishing of some sort. And that seems to be the bug with many antiques that are of unique form and structure. Many collectors are reluctant to acquire anything that can't be conveniently displayed on a wall, shelf, in a den corner or inside a trophy case.

But with museum groups avidly searching out and preserving the few remaining pack train relics, only the far-sighted collector will have secured one and provided for its appropriate display. In determining a fair trade value for one, $45 or $50 is not very far off. On this particular relic I can predict that the day isn't too far distant when they'll bring $85 to $100. They're closely linked to the days of the mountain men and the opening of the first trade routes in the far West. They're interesting and they're quite rare.

BARBED WIRE

AUTHENTIC OLD BARBED wire from frontier homesteads and ranges has certainly "arrived," so to speak, in attain-

12. An early sawbuck type pack saddle. Found in a northern California mountain area in 1960.

ing acceptance and recognition as true Frontier Americana. During the past couple of years, curators and museum directors have placed a special emphasis upon

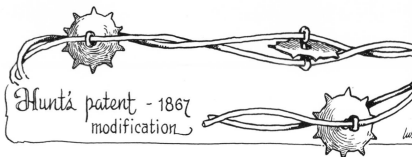

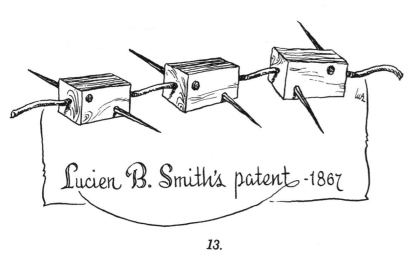

13.

14. Hunt's patent (Chester Hodge's modification)—1867.

the recovery and preservation of these fragments of pioneer development, for several types representing the earliest patents have all but disappeared.

I have spent the better part of my weekends these past few summers in combing the scrublands of western Kansas and along the Kansas-Nebraska border country in search of early types, and have come to realize that certain primitive, hand-produced examples are to be regarded in that same category of frontier relic as the buffalo skull or Colt Peacemaker.

Research discloses that the earliest patent for a wire

fence equipped with projecting points or barbs was issued to a Lucien B. Smith on June 25, 1867. His design consisted essentially of small wooden blocks encasing a stout wire. Through each block two sharp brads were driven, each in an opposing direction. Smith had hit upon a basic idea but he must have been a poor businessman because no fences were ever marketed which employed this principle of attaching barb to wire strand. I know of no existing example of his original model—there is merely the drawing which he submitted with his patent application.

Less than a month later, on July 23, a smithy named William D. Hunt secured a patent for a wire with a spurwheel or rowel attachment. This stuff was produced in a very limited quantity—less than one mile was manufactured. Hunt was without capital and the wire was costly to fabricate, so his venture soon fizzled. An investor named Charles Kennedy bought out Hunt's patent rights

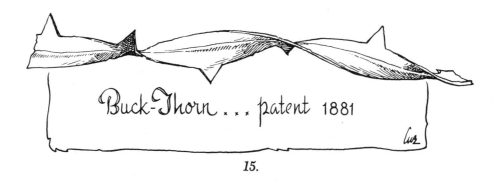

15.

for $175 and, after modifying the design somewhat, produced a fencing that actually saw use on many homesteads in western Kansas.

Kennedy's modification didn't work out too well, though. The spur-wheel wouldn't rotate properly around the wire and the hides of the critters became torn and scarred. Hide buyers and tanners growled about this so the wire was subjected to many modifications in an attempt to remedy the fault. Finally, Chester A. Hodge came along and rigged up the rowel on a sort of axle. This solved the problem. However, by that time (1887) other styles of barbs had captured a good bit of the trade. Hodge's stuff had arrived just a mite too late to make much of a dent in the market. I found a few feet of Hodge's modification near Holyrood, Kansas, recently—a rather thrilling discovery as this patent is a scarce type.

Now we come to the distinctive patent of an Irish farmer, Michael Kelly, who invented a flat, elongated diamond point which was so decidedly different from previous experimental types that it was granted a specific patent on February 11, 1868. He manufactured the wire under the name of Thorn Wire Hedge Company of Chicago, shipped it west, and was virtually without competition for a couple of years. This was the first commercially successful barbed wire enterprise and did much to establish barb as an effective means of keeping the "buffalo out and the cattle in."

Once the new fencing caught on, the frontier exploded with ingenious "bob-wire" devices intent upon claiming a share of the wealth from the booming cattle trade. Emphasis shifted to simplification of manufacture, stability and effectiveness of the barb itself, and the consequent lowering of cost to the rancher or sodbuster.

When the St. Louis and San Francisco Railroad fenced its right of way across Kansas, it utilized the infamous Buck-Thorn spiral wire, a vicious ribbon of sharp, lance-shaped points that caused a good bit of ill-feeling among the sodbusters who alleged that the product was too mean and cruel. Some attempts were made to have it outlawed because of the injury it could do to wayward critters; however, the animals soon learned to observe a healthy respect for it. I recently found a few feet of Buck-Thorn wrapped around an old fencepost near Marquette, Kansas, and I agree that the stuff is downright barbarous.

Perhaps the most successful of all barbed wire was the extremely simple two-point loop perfected by Joseph Glidden, an enterprising farmer, in 1876. Old Glidden had fiddled around for several years producing various pronged devices which he attached to interlaced strands of wire. He was striving for a simple, durable, non-rotating barb, because the chief fault with some of the older patents (buffalo wire is a good example), was that the beasts would frequently brush against the wire and loosen the barbs, causing them to rotate ineffectively around the strand. Glidden's innovation had a strong selling point in that it guaranteed a more permanent deterrent effect.

In my field trips searching for early frontier barb, I've come upon a few types which were apparently produced by foundries and metalsmiths in direct infringement upon the recognized patent holders' rights. These specimens reflect the extensive litigation and legal wranglings which resulted from the tidal wave of barbed wire production from 1873 to 1877. Some of these barb devices are truly classic and deserve a special niche in the collector's display case.

During the rash of new types of barb, the firm of Washburn and Moen quietly bought up the old patents and enjoyed something of a monopoly of the wire market for awhile. This situation created an entirely new field for enterprising smithies. They came out with hand machines and crimping tools suitable for attaching homemade barbs to spools of smooth wire. The courts held that this did not constitute a violation of patent rights since the fencing was not sold after home manufacture.

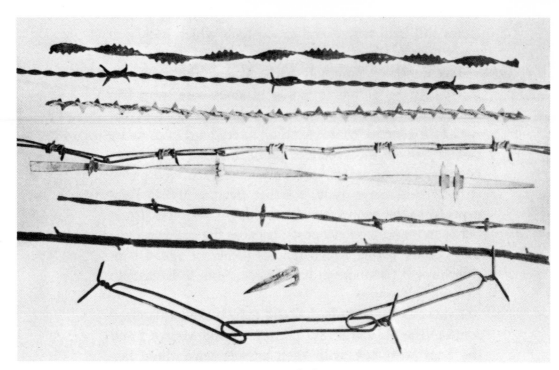

16. Frontier Barbed Wire

Reading from top to bottom:
1. *Sawtooth ribbon wire. Variation of Buck-Thorn patent—about 1881.*
2. *W. Watkins patent—1876.*
3. *Champion wire. Patented by E. M. Crandal in 1879. Sometimes called "ricrac" or "zigzag" barb.*
4. *One of J. W. Griswold's link-wire patents—about 1891.*
5. *Wire patented by J. Brinkerhoff in 1879.*
6. *D. C. Stover's wire. Heavy iron barb, apparently cast, clamped on— 1875.*
7. *Lyman P. Judson's 1871 patent. Rare.*
8. *Unusual nail for attaching barbed wire to fenceposts. Old and scarce.*
9. *Texas gate wire. Variation of patents by Griswold and E. L. Lewis. About 1891.*

Tool sheds on many old farms throughout the prairie states still hold rusted and pitted tools which had been used in rigging homemade barb.

The curious Champion barb, a sawtooth stamping laced between a double strand of stout wire, was, like some of the earlier patents, expensive to produce and met with little success, consequently it's very hard to come by now. In almost two years of probing midwestern range country, I've come up with only a ten-inch well-pitted strip of this scarce type. I rather imagine it has been exposed to the elements since the day it was first strung between limestone fenceposts, because the surfaces have that certain patina which reflects plenty of age. I consider myself fortunate in having been able to latch onto that meager example.

Lyman's four-point barb is still to be picked up around some of the old barns and pastures in the Midwest and the Southwest but, with each passing year, these fascinating bits of Americana are lost through deterioration and corrosion. My collection of some twenty-two types contains a dozen or so which simply couldn't be replaced without weeks, perhaps months, of diligent search. I doubt if Hodge's spur-wheel modification would show up for me again, as it's missing in many important historical society collections. Even Kelly's diamond-point is a twenty to one shot on a prairie expedition today.

Four or five years ago the pricing factors to be applied to old barbed wire specimens amounted to something of an unknown quantity because no one had done very much in determining the relative scarcity of some of the early patents. However, during the past year or so, a

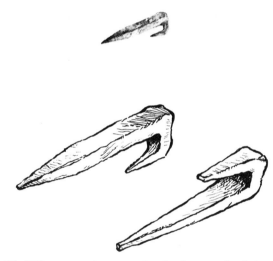

17. *Wherever frontier barbed wire had been strung, there's a possibility of finding a scarce, old nail like this. These hand-forged grip nails were the forerunner of the staples used to fasten wire of a later period.*

spirited fraternity of barbed wire collectors has sprung up and with the buying, selling, trading and diligent study of fence lore a much more realistic valuation can be assigned to the several collectable types.

The early experimental innovations (1867 to 1873) may be grouped into a class that rates $8 to $10 for an eighteen-inch example, the usual specimen length de-

sired by collectors. In display, this size will normally show two or three barbed devices and depict the spacing measurement between each. Patents after 1873 generally fall into the $3 to $4 per specimen category until we get to about 1890. After that, most patents amount to little more than harping on the same old theme and offer scant substance in the way of uniqueness or ingenuity of concept.

About thirty distinctive types serve to constitute a fairly comprehensive collection of early frontier wire. The year-span grouping and pricing indicated above holds true in most cases, but now and then a variable creeps in which makes it the exception rather than the rule. Take, for instance, the O. M. Pond patent of January 2, 1883. According to the patent date, it falls into the $3 to $4 bracket but this barb device was so zany in concept that it never did attain acceptance and is, consequently, rare and expensive. Same is true of some stuff created by a feller named L. Bagger in 1876. This, too, was a weird affair that never quite made the grade; a real tough one to come by and, of course, worth more.

For the most part, the years 1867 to 1873 may be considered the classic period. Values then string out downward to about $2.50 per specimen by the close of the era—1890.

So what does all this chatter about barbed wire lead up to? Simply this—many of these early types are becoming nonexistent, and the fact that antique dealers are displaying plaques of mounted barb indicates one thing—another utilitarian item of the frontier has caught the imagination of collectors.

I'll gladly trade my scarce Pothook and Turkey Track brand irons for a ten-inch strip of Hunt's *original* patent (not to be confused with the several modifications of the Hunt patent). Better latch on to all you can find of these "bits and pieces" relics of the West—they played a bigger part than most. "Bob-wire" ended the free range forever.

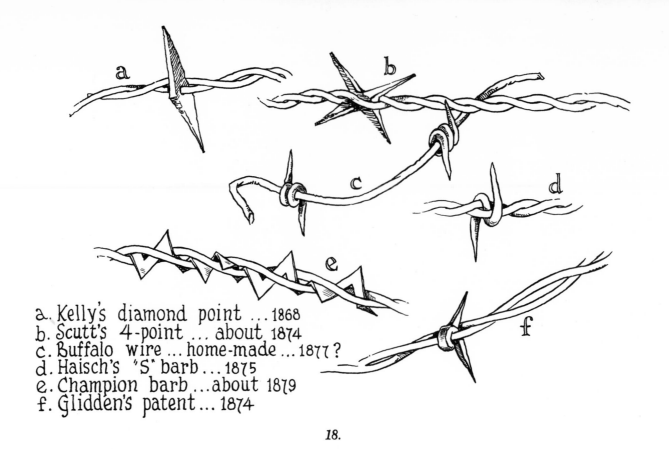

a. Kelly's diamond point ... 1868
b. Scutt's 4-point ... about 1874
c. Buffalo wire ... home-made ... 1877?
d. Haisch's "S" barb ... 1875
e. Champion barb ... about 1879
f. Glidden's patent ... 1874

18.

DEHORNING SAW

THE THING TO remember in probing around for an old dehorning saw or horn-tipper saw is that these tools are still made and used today so a fair measure of discernment will have to be exercised in order to authenticate an early one. By "early one," I mean one that dates from the late 1870s as there was little or no dehorning of critters on the open range during the era of the great cattle drives.

Dehorning saws were, following the fencing of the free range, quite essential for use at stock raising spreads and even around homestead pastures. Three or four types go to make up the entire crop of these things. A common one is the Ward horn-tipper, a stout sawblade fitted into a pistol-grip handle, very similar in overall appearance to a carpenter's runt-sized keyhole saw. Then there's a framed dehorning blade, almost identical to the ordinary hacksaw in its structural design. One other model is the knife-type saw, an ordinary sawtooth blade with a straight, butcher knife handle. Actually, there's nothing

very dramatic about any of them except that the acquisition of a circa 1880 example can pose a real challenge.

Here is where certain telltale characteristics will be of

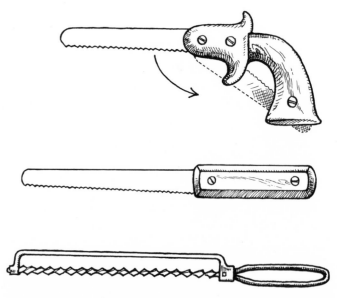

19. Dehorning saws: top, Ward horn-tipper; middle, knife handle; bottom, framed horn saw.

prime importance in determining the age of the tool. There's a kind of warmth—a mellowness—on the surface of old wood. Patina, it's called. So the wooden handle of a horn-tipper will have to be closely examined to detect the presence of that quality.

Some old dehorning saws have metal handles, but old metallic surfaces also bespeak a certain well-worn appearance that results from long exposure to country elements. It's simply a matter of acquainting the eye to the essential difference between an old bolt or door hinge or hammer head and its contemporary grandchild. I'm afraid there's no magic formula to apply here; it's sometimes a tough proposition to ascertain with absolute certainty that an object has all the earmarks to establish its antiquity or frontier heritage. But the practiced eye can usually sense the newness or oldness of these, as well as all other tools, blades, and implements. In brief, an educated eye is the only competent judge in the matter of aged wood, metal, leather, fabric or whatever the substance.

Tops for a tolerably good old dehorning saw is $6.

STIRRUPS

FOUR OR FIVE different types will suffice to cover the stirrups that were most common to the Plains. As in other items of horse gear, there were a dozen or more different designs in fairly general use during the past century but the ones dealt with here are probably the most typical—and they're all quite available to collectors today. This is accounted for by the simple fact that saddles were mighty durable, as well as costly, pieces of equipment, and were retained long after Old Paint had gone on to where all good horses go. Through disuse, saddle leather deteriorated but the old stirrups had a little longer lease on life and are still knocking around in some quantity. Hence, availability and tolerably reasonable prices.

As remarked, some five types will form a pretty comprehensive array. Here they are: the boxcar, doghouse, Visalia, oxbow and Turner. The latter is an iron job of a somewhat later period than the others—about 1900, to be exact. All of them come under a general classification called Rocky Mountain-Plains Stirrups, which adequately identifies their locale or regional background and also provides something of a key as to the trades in which they were engaged.

The boxcar, or box stirrup as it is sometimes called, is an adaptation of the old Spanish one-piece wooden stirrup. The tread on some of these old monstrosities is quite wide—about five inches. The overall character of this stirrup may best be described as "clumsy." But they were easy to make and attained a fairly wide acceptance by the American cowboy in spite of their ill-proportioned bulk. The *vaqueros* of the border country seemed to be tradition-bound in their tolerance of this stirrup design for they were used extensively by those cowhands long after the American riders had replaced them with ones of more practical size, shape and weight.

Another big, boxy affair, the doghouse, similarly reflects a strong Spanish influence. It, too, was quickly rejected by the Southwesterners when something better came along, but enough of them were prevalent throughout the West to make them hardly less common than the boxcar. The southwestern spreads had been manned with a good showing of Mexican riders and that's the principal reason this type stirrup shows up quite frequently these days.

Now we come to the Visalia, the most popular of all Plains stirrups. They were a sensible refinement of the older, boxy types that embodied all the good features of those forerunners with the added advantages of trimness, a much more practical flat tread or grip surface, and, of course, reduced weight. There are lots of them around **and anything over $10 for a nice, old pair should be regarded as outrageous.**

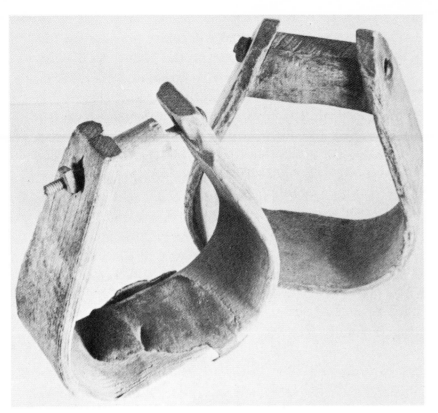

20. *Boxcars—usually called box stirrups. What's left of the rawhide tread on the one in the foreground certainly tells a story of many days on the trail.*

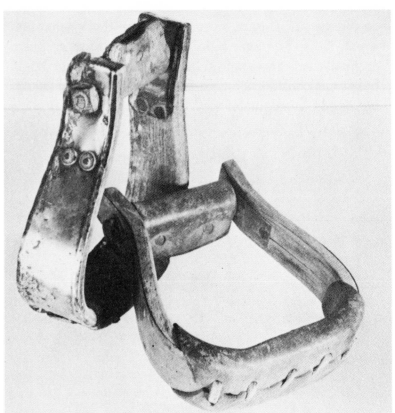

21. *The Visalia—one of the most popular of all western stirrup designs. The upright one has a light-gage brass facing; the other is faced with galvanized tin.*

Oxbow is an appropriate term for that stirrup as the slender, rounded proportions give it the appearance of being a miniature oxbow. These were the favorites of bronc busters and ropers who rode best with a full grip on the stirrup. They're more scarce than the Visalias and **worth $4 or $5 more, if in good shape.** Most of them originally had a rawhide reinforced tread, which should bear some consideration when the greenbacks are changing hands. It might be well to mention here that some boxcar and Visalia stirrups had hide treads—not all of them, but some—so completeness should be afforded a measure of regard when the price is discussed.

The Turner and its variants, cast iron stirrups with an oxidized tin rust-resistant finish, must be included although they never did make much of a dent in the western stirrup market. Their chief drawbacks were in their excessive weight and the fact that during winter range work they were awfully doggone cold. The only asset, if such there be, was that they didn't break, but this virtue didn't serve to contribute much toward their favor in the cattle country. If you find a pair and simply can't resist **their offbeat appeal, $7.50 should do it.**

Just for good measure, I'm throwing in the military stirrup. At the termination of the Civil War, a vast horde of ex-cavalrymen and homestead-seeking veterans of all sorts fanned out westward, many of them bringing their service mounts and military hoss gear with them. Add to this the twenty-odd year postwar span during which the U. S. Cavalry was active at the frontier outposts and you have a mighty big passel of old bits, spurs and stirrups lurking around the great West.

Confederate stirrups are scarce as hen's teeth and when one does show up, the Civil War buffs bid it up well nigh out of reach in short order. But there are still some with the "U.S." and similar quartermaster stampings and indicia to be had. On the antique market, officers' models, usually of brass, have always been priced higher than the iron stirrups that were issued to enlisted troopers. This pricing criteria seems to me to be faulty as

22. Oxbow stirrup.

I've seen far less iron stirrups than brass, notwithstanding the fact that there were undoubtedly more mounted enlisted men than officer personnel. I think the price tags should be switched around because the better crafted, polished brass models were apparently more subject to retention than the rust-prone iron models. So in this case I would re-align the established pricing index to provide for a $20 tag on the iron pair and $15 to $18 for the brass. Some dealers may develop tight jaws over this assertion but until I learn of an old government warehouse disposal sale that includes a sizable lot of old enlisted issue stirrups, the value factor cited will have to stand pat.

BRIDLE BITS

Snaffles, spades, ring bits, hackarees, military, bar bits, Visalia humane bits—all styles and forms of mouthpieces will be encountered by the collector in his search for examples of these essential items of hoss gear. Contrivances for controlling horses date pretty far back into

23. Cast iron stirrup—Turner pattern.

history—along about 4000 B.C., to be fairly accurate, when the Scythians used horses to draw their chariots. Down through the centuries the means of guiding and controlling horses evolved into some of the types we see today. There's a linked snaffle bit that was used by the ancient Greeks which is almost a dead ringer for the ones used on farm horses (where there are farm horses) at present. Seems as if the U. S. Patent Office granted approval to just about every single applicant who submitted a bit design even though the principle or function of the mouthpiece was no different than a dozen other such types. A mere variation of a couple degrees in the slant of the cheek pieces or a quarter-inch difference in the breadth of the bar span was sufficient to qualify it as a new shape. This patent liberality accounts for the

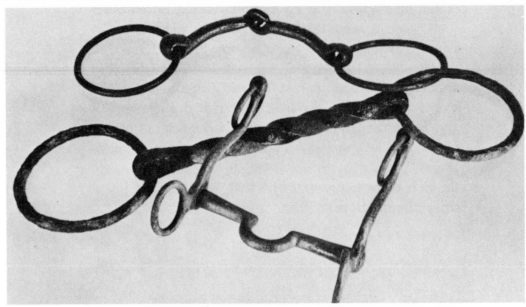

24. Old bits. The snaffle or linked bit (upper), bar bit and Texas Model were all prevalent throughout the West.

scores of types that flooded the market during the '70s and '80s, although few, if any, provided much in the way of practical advantage over others previously introduced. It was largely a matter of catering to the horseman's taste through those minor variables that made one bit just a little different from another.

Anyway, bits have been around as long as hosses so it's virtually impossible to cover much more than a few representative types that were in general use on the range during the past hundred years or so.

Simple, plain snaffles were quite prevalent everywhere in the West. They are a general utility type of bit, not exactly gentle and not what you'd call severe—a good "happy medium" sort of bit. That's why they were so favored by sodbusters and farmers.

Spade bits and ring bits are much more severe. They were utilized to a great extent on the early cattle spreads where immediate response by half-wild horses was man-datory.

There's a bit called the Texas Model which has had a wide acceptance by cowhands because of the sensible, short-shanked cheek piece (light weight) and the fact that it's easy on the horse's mouth. This bit is the outcome of that later period in western history when the cow ponies were afforded longer periods of training and consequently required far less severe methods to compel obedience.

So, wherever there were horses, there were bits and there is hardly an old barn, stable or wagon shed that won't yield at least one of the more common types if a feller probes around long enough. Snaffles are worth $2.50, maybe $3—no more. Nice Texas Models bring $7.50 to $10 and the other, fancier jobs—those of Spanish influence with ornate jingle chains and cricket rollers—bring $20 and upwards, depending upon age and condition.

TABLE OF VALUES

The column on the right denotes the degree of scarcity of each relic. The numbers assign a scarcity factor as follows: 1–3 common, 4–6 scarce, 7–9 rare.

Relic	Fair	Good	Excellent	Scarcity Factor
Barbed Wire—18″ Span				
Patents:				
1867–1873	$ 4	$ 6	$ 8–10	6
1874–1890	$ 2	$ 3	$ 4–4.50	4
Bridle Bits				
Early Spanish	$12.50	$16	$ 20+	7
Snaffles	$ 1.50	$ 2.50	$ 3	1
Spade and Ring	$ 7.50	$12	$ 15+	5–6
Texas Model	$ 4	$ 6.50	$ 8–10	4
Dehorning Saws				
Wards Horn-tipper	$ 3	$ 4.50	$ 6	3
Framed or Knife	$ 3	$ 4	$ 5–6	3
Oxshoe	$ 1.50	$ 2	$ 3	2
Ox Yokes				
Double	$20–25	$60	$ 75+	6
Single	$30	$65+	$ 85+	7
Pack Saddle	$25	$35–40	$ 50+	6
Stirrups—Pairs				
Boxcar	$ 7.50	$ 9	$ 12	5
Doghouse	$ 7.50	$ 9	$ 10–12	4–5
Military:				
Confederate	$20	$25+	$ 40+	8
Union:				
Brass	$10	$14	$ 17.50	6
Iron	$12	$17.50	$ 20+	7
Oxbow	$ 9	$12	$ 15	6
Turner	$ 3	$ 6	$ 8	4
Visalia	$ 5	$ 7.50	$ 10	2

AT THE MINER'S SHACK

25. *A street scene in the mining town of Wickes, Montana, by an unknown frontier photographer. The merchants' signs are quite interesting, particularly the watchmaker's emblem suspended near the center of the picture.*

CANDLESTICK

THE SPIKED GADGET pictured here is called a miner's candlestick and hardly needs much in the way of explanation. Once a feller dug his way a few yards into the side of a mountain, he needed light and this type of candlestick was designed to provide for that requirement. A candle was inserted in the cupped receptacle; the thing was stuck into a timber or shoring post or between rock crevices and that was that. These candlesticks were used only in mines, so far as I've been able to learn, so they qualify fully as items related to the lore of the bonanzas.

The illustration is a clip from a 1903 wholesale hardware catalog of the Norvell-Shapleigh Hardware Company of St. Louis, Missouri. The company had been established long prior to that date, however, and a good many gross of these candleholders were transported by freighters into the mining districts during the '50s and '60s. The price shown in the catalog provides an interesting sidelight—$1. This particular model even had a trade moniker of its own. It was listed as "The Miner's Favorite," which the maker probably felt was a real wingding merchandising pitch.

When I was in England a few years ago, I saw an identical one on Portobello Road, a flea market district in London. Seems as if these things really got around and it's entirely possible that the ones wholesaled by Norvell-Shapleigh were European imports. Anyway, the grouchy

26. Miner's Candlestick.

old cuss who operated the flea market stall (he had an aversion to Yankee accents) caustically told me that these candlesticks were used in the Welsh mines and that each miner owned his own candlestick—same as his lunch pail. They were not items of company property. Can't recall exactly what the price was—two or three shillings, I think—about 35¢. But that old bloke was a downright discourteous sort; my indignation was greater than my desire to own the relic, so I left his stall without it.

In the adventurous world of junk shops, musty cellars, attics, flea markets, abandoned barns, and all the fascinating places where these treasures abound, the collector will experience both triumph and boo-boos. When I got sore at the cantankerous old bloke in London it cost me a nice old miner's candlestick. These things are selling for **$12 and $15 now. Oh well . . .**

Obviously, you won't find these relics in prairie country or along the southwestern border. They're a sort of California or Nevada type of thing and there possibly are some knocking around Montana or in other northwestern areas where deep mining operations were conducted. Mostly, though, they're to be found in areas where Orientals were employed as mine laborers. In other words, they're a regional relic rather than the sort of thing you might find anywhere in the West. It's reasonable to assume that an OK Ranch spur might somehow have been transported to Iowa but man yokes just aren't the type of gear that people moved very far outside the mining communities.

Relics of this sort are by no means common. As in all

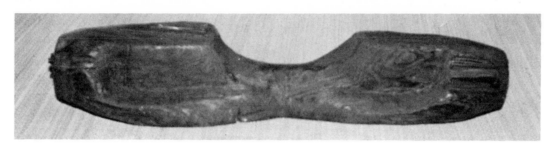

27. Man yoke.

MAN YOKE

MAN YOKES ARE age-old totin' devices so it's not in the least surprising that they were utilized to some extent during the great bonanzas in the Mother Lode country. The one in the illustration is a right nice example of the hand-fashioned ones that were used by Chinese laborers to carry ore-laden buckets from mine corridors to the main tunnels where the rich rock was emptied into ore carts for transport out of the mine. On this one the buckets were suspended from stout ropes fastened to the ends of the span. Some were equipped with iron hooks, loops or rings to accommodate the rope sling.

objects that are hand-crafted, no two are exactly alike and the criterion of value must necessarily be flexible. In large measure, the whittle marks or hatchet chip characteristics of the piece and the overall soundness and completeness of the metal fittings are essential to reasonable appraisal.

If crudely crafted, the relic is, understandably, less desirable than one that has been painstakingly whittled out and fitted with neat little wrought iron eyelets or hooks. Research reveals that some Chinese mine laborers carved their own yokes with special care to the shaping of the shoulders for a custom fit. Others were made on contract by town woodworkers to a somewhat standard set of specifications.

Let's say $20 to $25 for a really nice old man yoke.

POKE

THE PROSPECTOR'S POKE is an interesting fragment of the old mining frontier. The one shown here is of buckskin, about six inches long, barely two inches wide, with a wrap-around drawstring—entirely handmade, of course. Pokes such as this are pretty scarce since there was little or no practical usage for them other than that for which they were originally intended—to stash gold dust. The high mortality rate on these relics may be attributed to two factors: first, if the prospector struck it rich, he had no further use for the doggone thing and promptly discarded it; second, if he fared poorly, the poke would

seldom find its way into repose as a family heirloom.

At any rate, they're scarce. Can't recall that I've seen more than half a dozen genuine ones in that many years. Poke bags are not to be confused with the little buckskin money bags, mostly of commercial manufacture, which were in common use everywhere during the last century. Money pouches are usually bulb-shaped affairs with brass beads on the tips of the drawstrings.

Everytime I see one of these old pokes and analyze the homely concept of their makeup, I wonder why in the dickens a feller would decorate one. Yet, some have shown up with scrawly inscriptions, monograms, and other fanciful designs which I figure can only be ascribed to the length of the winter evenings when the old prospector had little else to do. This is purely speculative and probably amounts to some amateur psychology, I suppose. But pokes weren't for flashing around at frontier bars so the decorated ones do have a little extra story to

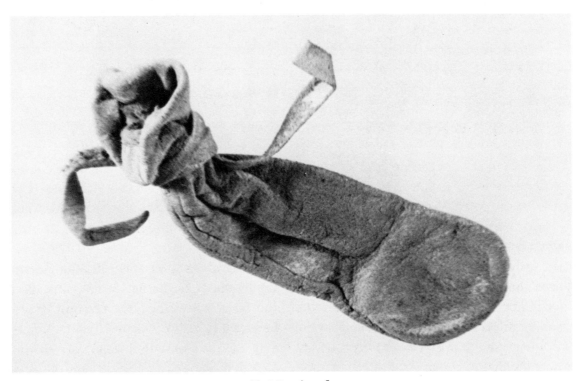

28. Miner's poke.

tell. The ratio of undecorated to decorated bags is possibly two to one which simply means that a fancy one is worth more.

A tolerably nice poke is worth around $20 and could very well be worth twice that amount when the true scarcity of these little rascals is eventually realized.

PAN AND QUARTZ PICK

GENERAL STORES OF a century ago stocked all kinds of pots and pans but not just any old baking pan, basin or dishpan can qualify as a prospector's pan. Although miner's pans were made in different sizes and of different metals, there is a definite characteristic in the gently sloped sides that readily distinguishes a real miner's pan from all other types of household "pannery."

The one shown here was recently found at Hangtown, California. It depicts quite well the shallow depth and modest taper of the pan walls and also the absence of an abrupt, rimmed edge. All these features served to render this piece of equipment expressly suitable to the function for which it was employed. In order to wash out the gravel and coarse sand from a gold bearing creek bed, the prospector had to manipulate the pan with a wrist action that would create a regulated swirling of the water. The shape of the pan played a pretty vital part in achieving that end result. So, to put it briefly, the miner's pan had to be shaped in such a manner as to afford a good measure of control to the swirling pattern of the water.

Seems as if all the blacksmiths and tinsmiths in the West got into the act when the fanatical demand for pans, picks, shovels and pry bars created the biggest pandemonium that had ever occurred on the old frontier. They used everything they could lay their hands on in order to forge these implements. I've seen miner's pans of heavy gauge tin, a couple of copper, several of light gauge iron, and even one of zinc.

The average diameter of these pans was somewhere in the neighborhood of eighteen inches. A good many of them are of machine manufacture—those that came along when the gold rush had gotten into high gear. But now and then one is recovered that has an impressed

29. *Miner's pan and quartz pick with fragments of gold bearing rock.*

"touch" or mark on the underside which identifies the individual metalsmith who fashioned it. These are the real prizes, invariably the earlier ones, and call for a healthy premium over the ones of later, machine production.

What has been remarked about the prospector's pan is pretty much the same story for the quartz pick, except that they were more the craft of the blacksmith rather than the town or itinerant tinsmith. Consequently, they seldom bear identifying marks or symbols.

About $20 to $22.50 for a good prospector's pan. Badly dented, rusted or otherwise serious deterioration puts it

30. Although the earliest mining equipment did not include any of the tools shown here (the Bowie knife was first used to dig the precious, gleaming flakes from crevices in rocks along the river banks), the pick, shovel and pan brought riches to many.

into a class where it probably can be bargained for at around $8 or $10. Same is true for the quartz pick, the bosom pal of the prospector's pan. They are equal in scarcity and value.

TABLE OF VALUES

The column on the right denotes the degree of scarcity of each relic. The numbers assign a scarcity factor as follows: 1–3 common, 4–6 scarce, 7–9 rare.

Relic	Fair	Good	Excellent	Scarcity Factor
Candlestick	$ 8	$12	$ 15	3
Man Yoke	$10	$16–18	$ 25	6
Pan				
Early	$12	$18	$ 22.50	8
Late	$10	$14	$ 18	6
Quartz Pick	$10	$14	$ 18.50	6
Poke				
Decorated	$10	$16	$ 20+	7
Plain	$ 8	$14	$ 17.50	6

AT THE GUNSMITH'S SHOP

Into town from the south.

31.   The above illustration was done in 1903 while Wyeth was still a student at Howard Pyle's studio. It shows the Daltons coming into quiet, prosperous Coffeyville on the morning of their famous bank robbery there. One of the earliest and rarest Wyeth "Westerns." Frank Leslie's Popular Monthly, *July, 1903.*

GUNSMITH'S SIGN

OLD TRADESMEN'S SIGNS have always had a broad appeal to collectors because of the quaintness, originality and artistic vigor that is so frequently evident in them. Many of them exemplify, to a marked degree, the art of wood carving, metal sculpture, painting, and all the allied creative specialities that flourished during those days when pride of craftsmanship was every tradesman's hallmark. They are actually one of the truest forms of folk art.

Good examples are scarce, bordering on rare. This is the result of interior decorators having snapped them up during the past several years to use as wall plaques along with trotting horse weather vanes, fire marks and similar creations of pioneer artisans. Even the plainer shop signs, without scrolled borders and heavily serifed Gothic lettering which was in vogue many years ago, are seldom found anymore. Real old tavern and ship chandler's signs are virtually impossible to locate.

I'm not convinced that tradesmen's signs are entirely extinct, though. When one considers the fact that every frontier community had a cobbler, harnessmaker, tinsmith, saddler, blacksmith, carriagemaker, watchmaker, liquor merchant, hatter, and scores of other mercantile establishments that displayed emblems of this sort—well there just *must* be more of them stashed away somewhere.

The gunsmith's emblem pictured here is a humdinger

and, insofar as frontier folk art is concerned, rates nothing short of the term "masterpiece." It is so wonderfully crafted that the best way to point out its qualities is to make a comparison with other forms of merchants' signs or emblems which the collector may come upon from time to time.

Just about the most common one is the blacksmith's symbol—the horseshoe—usually fashioned of sheet metal and suspended from a bracket over the double-door shop entrance. The simple shape of a horseshoe was easy to re-create in cutout form, so no great sculptural effort or artistic skill was required to produce one. Hence, there's not too much in the way of dimensional features about them. Town watchmakers displayed the typical pocket watch emblem. Some of these boasted a fair measure of dimensional effect, particularly in the watch stem or perhaps a few links of chain with fob attached. The cobblers had a boot or shoe to denote their craft and wares, but most of these were flat cutouts from board panels with scant attempt to dramatize the object through molded or realistic shaping.

That's what makes this gunsmith's emblem such a remarkable example. Examine the detailing closely. It was probably made by the gunsmith himself because the pistol frame is hand-forged wrought iron with great attention devoted to the actual proportions of the six-

32. For many years, this fine old gunsmith's emblem hung in front of a shop in southeastern Kansas. Completely handmade, it is a choice collectors' item.

shooter it sought to represent. The bored barrel, fitted cylinder and wooden grips give the weapon an authenticity that would have made old Sam Colt right proud. It would take very little more to rig it for shooting.

For many years this emblem or sign hung over the doorway of a gunsmith's shop in southeastern Kansas. I think it's by far the most intriguing and superbly crafted old frontier sign I've ever seen—worth every bit of a hundred-dollar bill. There are some relics that don't rightfully deserve the extra couple of "hurtin'" dollars it takes to acquire them, but an old gunsmith's sign isn't one of those relics.

Most collectors will have to settle for less. As remarked, the majority of signboards or emblems will be non-dimensional, that is, flat cutouts, so I wouldn't go much over $35 for one. But, if you should stumble on to an old rifle, wagon or likker keg sign that is sculptured or dimensional, whatever you choose to call this form of realism, you're dealing with a prize that ought not to be passed up. Those few extra dollars may "hurt" a mite at the time of the transaction. However, a month or so will soften the blow to a bright realization that the few extra bucks involved brought home an irreplaceable frontier relic. In short, don't lose a wonderful old emblem or sign if the price appears to be kind of dear because, scarcity criteria considered, it probably isn't.

HENRY RIFLE

I SHOULD EXPLAIN before we get into this business of rifles

and revolvers that no attempt can possibly be made here to provide much more than sketchy comments concerning the origin and significance of a few representative guns that figured mightily on the old frontier. Also, the rarity and pricing of them must be trod upon *very* gingerly. The reason for such deviation from the pattern of other chapters in this book is because old guns are a highly specialized subject unto themselves, towering head and shoulders above all other items of Frontier Americana. Public library shelves are stacked to the eaves with extremely comprehensive works on the historical background and value of antique arms. Their prices fluctuate almost from month to month. A half-dozen fine gun magazines hit the newsstands regularly so I'm certain the collector will realize that a few old guns are appropriate to this book, but the full story must be gleaned from other extensive and competent sources.

If you were to have peered over the shoulder of an old western gunsmith, there's a good possibility you would have looked at the innards of a .44 caliber Henry rifle. The principal feature of this gun is the magazine and the manner of loading from it. It consisted of a metal tube

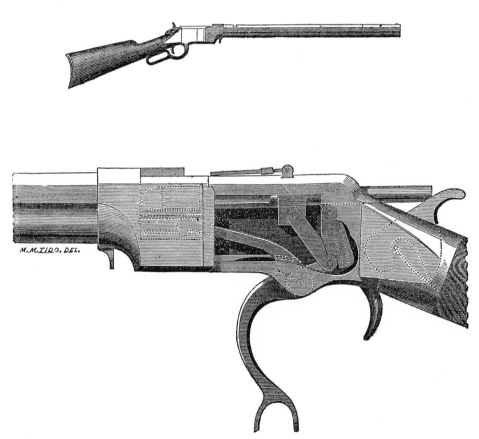

M. M. JIRO. DEL.

Sectional view of working parts, showing the operation of removing the empty cartridge and cocking the hammer.

33. Wood engravings from an 1862 publication show the breech mechanism and profile characteristics of the earliest Henry model.

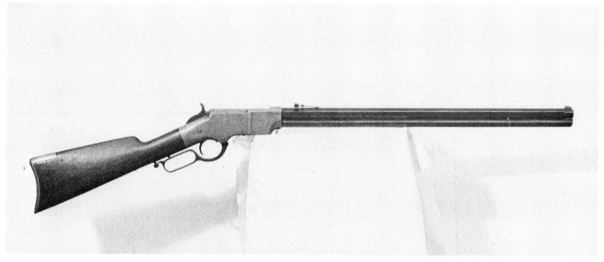

34. Forerunner of the Winchester, the Henry rifle saw service in the Civil War and on the western frontier. Cartridges fired by this weapon are still occasionally picked up around old camp sites.

under a 24-inch barrel, extending its entire length, of sufficient diameter to admit fifteen rimfire cartridges freely. A section of this tube near the muzzle contains a spiral spring to throw the cartridges upon a carrier block in the rear. By means of a five-inch metallic sleeve embracing the barrel of the gun at this point, it can be revolved upon the axis of the bore so as to open the magazine and admit the introduction of the cartridges. Upon closing it after filling, the spring throws a cartridge upon the carrier block, which, by a forward movement of the trigger guard, is raised to a level with the chamber. The hammer, by the same movement, is carried to a full cock. A reverse movement of the guard, bringing it to its place again, forces the cartridge into the chamber and the gun is ready to fire.

The ammunition is fixed, metal-cased, with fulminate or cap in the rear. The hammer, upon falling, strikes a rod or breechpin on the front of which are two sharp points which are driven into the rear of the cartridge, thus exploding it.

All this technical data may appear to be ponderous. However, this rifle, patented in 1860, was, in effect, the real grandpappy of all our repeating rifles and the principles of its mechanism do have a substantial claim to fame from a historical point of view. The tremendous increase in firepower of this rifle and its successor, the Winchester .66 "Yellow Boy," over the old single-shot breechloaders had a good deal to do with changing a lot of environmental conditions out West. The Henry rifle had an influence far out of proportion to its limited production—only 1731 saw Civil War service. But, this ten-pound weapon, with its 295 grain cartridges, wrote some vivid pages in frontier history.

B. Tyler Henry's rimfire metallic cartridge, and the amazing weapon which fired it, contributed enormously to the saga of Oliver Winchester's success and to the subsequent development of all repeating arms. The Henry rifle and its Winchester offspring completely revolutionized Plains warfare and brought an entirely different complexion to the face of the Old West. B. Tyler, sir, yours was a job well done! And, Ollie, you shore knew a good thing when you saw it!

SMITH AND WESSON AMERICAN

SOME FORTY-ODD years ago, the neighborhood gang and I tore around backyards in many a thrilling game of cops

that the Smith and Wesson #3 was every bit as significant on the western scene as was the Colt .45.

It's really strange how a certain product or model will assume a position of preeminence and be identified almost exclusively with a subject when, in reality, the item is but one of many. So often in western literature and illustration, the gun play simply isn't considered properly depicted unless the Peacemaker is brought to bear. Or, if

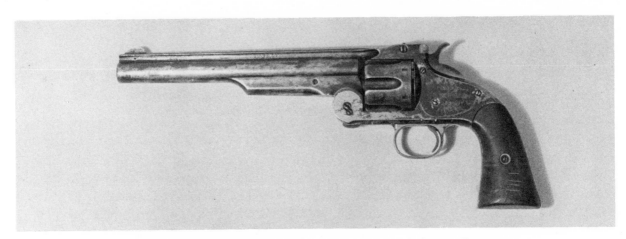

35. This Smith and Wesson American bears the inscription "Texas Jack Cottonwood Spring 1872." It was one of his most prized possessions. Issued as the #3 American .44 caliber, it was the first revolver using metallic ammunition issued to troops in the field. The barrel is stamped "U.S." and the serial number is 2008.

and robbers. Invariably, the good guys pretended to be shooting it out with their Smith and Wesson .38 Police Specials. For a long time I had the notion that the only thing Smith and Wesson ever produced was a police revolver, because that particular model was something of a standard side arm for law enforcement officers in big cities everywhere at the time.

However, the firm of Smith and Wesson had done right well for itself in the old western gun market, too. As a matter of fact, when I got around to something resembling a serious look at the early western arsenal, I found

rifles are involved, it just *has* to be a Winchester. I don't mean to infer that the Colts, Winchesters and Deringers weren't mighty important pieces of equipment in the arsenal of the Old West. But how often do you read of a frontier marshal drawing his .44 American or his .36 Remington?

The Smith and Wesson folks came out with the first metallic cartridge revolvers during the Civil War and, as early as 1871, the #3 American was in the hands of troops at frontier outposts. This weapon was a revolutionary breakthrough in the development of side arms and hundreds of them saw service at remote western sites a good while before the Peacemaker or Frontier Model arrived on the scene in 1874. Buffalo Bill carried a Smith and Wesson .44; so did his associate, the famous scout, Texas Jack Omohundro. My good friend, Herschel C. Logan of Santa Ana, California, now owns Jack's fine old pistol.

In viewing museum exhibits and historical collections during the past few years, I've found that these Smith and Wessons are almost as prevalent in gun cabinets displaying frontier relics as are the Colts and Winchesters. This pretty well bears out my assertion that S & W pistols had a bigger role in the western panorama than many folks might suppose. What I mean to convey here is that gunsmoke from a #3 American has just as much western

pungence as many other big names and models. If you were to peer again over the shoulder of the old gunsmith, chances are good he'd be working on one. The little S & W trademark might very well have been the symbol for "Strictly Western."

SPENCER CARBINE

LET'S PEEK OVER that gunsmith's shoulder again. This time he has taken down a .50 caliber Spencer carbine and the innards will give us a pretty fair idea as to why this weapon was considered by military experts to be the best carbine used by either side during the Civil War.

36. *A Spencer carbine in an original saddle holster. This weapon was considered by military experts as the best carbine used on either side during the Civil War. Later, they were issued to rail-laying crews on the Kansas Pacific Railroad for protection against marauding bands.*

The magazine is in the breech of the gun and the metallic cartridges are fed into the chamber successively by means of a spiral spring. The breechblock was operated by the trigger guard which, when swung down, acted as a lever to open the breech, eject a spent cartridge, and then position a new one into the barrel from the tubular magazine in the butt. The tin tube containing seven cartridges provided a rapid fire capability that was a tremendous advance over the other multishot rifles and carbines that were introduced along about this time—1860.

Mass produced during the War, a good many of them found their way westward after Appomattox and took their places alongside the Henrys, Sharps and Winches-ters as a general purpose sort of firearm. The Spencer carbine weighed ten pounds and originally sold for $38.

Soon after it was patented, military tests were conducted to evaluate its effectiveness. Results: ninety-nine shots in eight minutes and twenty seconds, loading time included! That's a heap of .50 caliber delivery for a circa 1860 shootin' iron. Old Spencer himself got off nine shots in one minute, loading the last two cartridges individually, in demonstrating his own test rifle.

Yep! Those old Spencers blasted off a right sizable payload. They did more than a mere trifle to push that old frontier a mite farther westward. A dad-burned fine old gun.

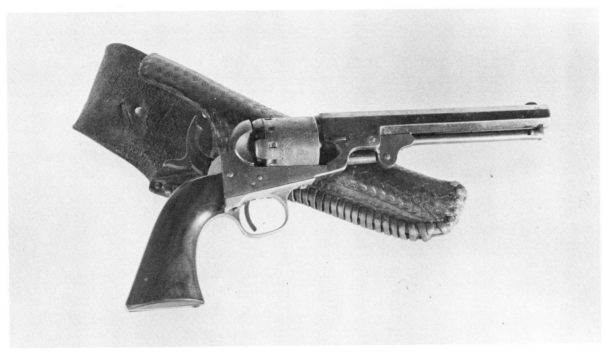

37. This excellent .36 caliber Manhattan cap and ball five-shooter, with its old style holster, was the side arm of a Civil War soldier who later busted sod in central Kansas. It is almost an exact copy of Colt's 1851 Navy model.

.36 CALIBER CAP AND BALL PISTOL

OLD CAP AND ball pistols were the principal side arm of the Westerner for a period of thirty years or more preceding the development of the metallic cartridge.

Sam Colt started off the entire affair back in the 1840s when the Texas Rangers got to using his earliest revolving pistols with a mighty impressive degree of effectiveness. During the Civil War gunmakers far and wide jumped on the bandwagon to produce side arms for the military forces, a good many of these weapons being dead ringers of the ones old Sam Colt had come up with some years earlier. That's what this .36 caliber Navy model Manhattan cap and ball pistol is—a dead steal of Colt's 1851 Navy model. It's a quality firearm, nonetheless, having been made to the most exacting standards and delivered to the U. S. Ordnance Department in 1863.

I came by my .36 caliber Manhattan cap and ball five-shooter via a rather circuitous route. In relating how it wound up in my display case, the collector should get a fair idea of how he might employ items that are somewhat foreign to his collecting interest as stepping stones toward an item he needs or wants. To swap effectively, you sometimes have to map out a route that will take you across three or four traders' tables. Here's how my gun deal worked out:

I heard about the feller, an avid Confederate States postage stamp collector, who owned this pistol. It had been the side arm of his great-grandpappy during the Civil War. After Appomattox, the old soldier had turned sodbuster and toted it into Kansas.

In the course of my ramblings and probings over the years, I had accumulated a lot of bric-a-brac which didn't tie in much with my frontier stuff. However, I could swap a passel for other things I didn't need which could, in turn, be swapped for stamps—but not Confederate stamps. Briefly, one big parcel of unrelated, unwanted items went for another stack of unusables which went for some precancelled stamps—valuable, rare ones. I unloaded the precancels to a stamp dealer for some top notch Confederate stamps which brought home the pistol. And it is a beauty!

At the time of our transaction (1962), the stamps were worth close to $100. The pistol is now worth $250. Maybe the stamps are presently worth more, but so what? My swap objective was achieved and this ole .36 caliber cap and ball looks awfully nice in my gun cabinet. And I'm sure the Confederate stamps look right nice in the other feller's album.

Come to think of it, Jerry displayed those Confederate States stamps at a tri-state philatelic exhibition not long ago and came off with a top award. So the overall result of that hoss-tradin' enterprise has had a real happy effect on both of us. I believe this is the sensible way to trade. Both fellers afford a just consideration for each other's collection; neither party experiences a belated disappointment because of disproportionate value received; and each collection is measurably enhanced by the new acquisition.

THE PEACEMAKER

GUESS I SHOULD begin with the phrase, "Last, but by no means least . . ." for the Colt Peacemaker, or Frontier Model or 1873 Colt (whatever the collector chooses to call this renowned weapon) was the last of those distinguished firearms to be closely linked with the Old West. However, it was far from being least in preeminence.

Sam Colt had been dead some ten years when this fine revolver made its appearance. By virtue of old Sam's reputation in the development and production of fine revolving pistols, this handgun didn't have to get out there and do much in the way of proving itself in order to attain acceptance. Colt's name was enough. The Army

38. *Brought out in 1873, this Frontier Model Colt is stamped "U.S."*
It saw plenty of service on the frontier.

bought 8,000 almost before the factory had a chance to set up for production. In short, everybody knew this revolver *had* to be good—and it was.

It was chambered for different calibers but the regular model was a .45 caliber, single action six-shooter with a barrel length of seven and one-half inches. To extol its merits to any great extent would be repetitious of what has been said a thousand and one times in dozens of articles, features and books dealing with firearms and frontier history. Let's condense all that verbiage into one concise summation: This revolver was a doggone good piece of lead-slingin' hardware.

But I have a bone to pick from a dollars and cents point of view. I don't want to alienate the affections of Colt collectors and generate a controversy by stating that this enduring weapon is overpriced and, therefore, a poor investment. This may sound like a paradox; but many Colt Peacemakers *are* overpriced and, also, *are* a good investment.

For example, my wife is presently toying with the idea of shelling out $85 for a late Victorian parlor lamp she spotted in a local antique shop. The lamp is an attractive thing and possesses a right smart passel of decorative virtues. It's one of many, many thousands that were mass produced during the 1880s and 1890s—a volume type of merchandise that originally sold for $8 or $10. But the charm and ornamental qualities of these lamps have created such a spirited demand for them, that the prices are far in excess of their true antiquarian worth. The old law of supply and demand so merchandising experts say.

There are a thousand of them on shopkeepers' shelves with two thousand customers clamoring at the doors. So it is with the Peacemaker. This model was produced in huge quantities, year after year, until the 1900s when the automatics began to get a toehold on the pistol market. I do feel that many of these six-shooters, particularly those with serial numbers in the umpteen thousands, bear price tags that are quite inconsistent with some of the hard rules that ought to apply. Nevertheless, like those Victorian parlor lamps, they're a good investment because folks continue to be enchanted with them and the price goes up and up making 'em more valuable in the process.

The earliest production of these fine revolvers (the low serial number jobs) are doggone near worth what's asked for them. They're the true classics of this series and come fairly close to warranting the extra dollars on their price tags. But for the life of me, I can't quite see those thousands of Frontier Models, which never saw service outside Baltimore, Bangor or Sheboygan, being afforded nearly the same degree of acclaim as the early Army issue. No one seems to want to separate the men from the boys I guess. Maybe this is as it should be. I'm still not completely converted to the offbeat situation, although I did tell the wife to go ahead and buy that lamp. In spite of the crazy market, it's a dingbusted good investment.

TABLE OF VALUES

The column on the right denotes the degree of scarcity of each relic. The numbers assign a scarcity factor as follows: 1–3 common, 4–6 scarce, 7–9 rare.

Relic	Fair	Good	Excellent	Scarcity Factor
Colt .45 (Frontier Model) single action with 7½" barrel— "U.S." marked	$ 95	$175	$250+	6
Gunsmith's Sign				
dimensional	$ 40	$ 60	$ 90+	8
nondimensional	$ 15	$ 25	$ 35	5
Henry Rifle (exceedingly rare with iron frame)	$200	$400	$575	8
Manhattan .36 Caliber Cap and Ball Five-Shooter	$ 90	$165	$250	6
Smith and Wesson American ("U.S." marked)	$150	$200	$275–300	8
Spencer Carbine	$ 90	$125	$175+	5

AT THE FRONTIER OUTPOST

39. N. C. Wyeth painted this cavalry officer and his orderly as an illustration for Scribner's Magazine in 1907. Even in this relatively minor work, Wyeth has characterized two distinct personalities; the erect, austere, rigid formality of the commander and the relaxed, casual attitude of the old enlisted trooper.

THE SIBLEY STOVE

HERE IS A military-frontier relic that is really a unique contraption. Sibley stoves (homely little bed-tent heaters of Civil War vintage) have quite an interesting background and deserve much broader recognition as items of Frontier Americana than has heretofore been afforded them.

This funnel-shaped stove was invented by an old-time Dragoon officer, Major Henry Hopkins Sibley, as an accessory to his campaign tent—the Sibley—for use by military detachments in the field. Sibley, a West Pointer (Class of 1838), had accompanied Fremont on one of his expeditions in the West and had noted the advantages of the Plains Indian's tepee. One could hardly credit the Major with exercising brilliant ingenuity or resourcefulness in developing his tent design since it was nothing more than a canvas adaptation of the wigwam. However, the old boy came up with something special when he devised the little cone-shaped tent warmer. Nothing could have been more simple to construct, more practical to use, or lighter to transport than the bottomless sheet iron stove which he patented in 1857.

The standard model Sibley stove was an airtight cylinder thirty inches tall with an eighteen-inch base diameter. A small, semi-circular opening at the bottom served to provide draft and, when the draft required checking, the trooper merely kicked a little pile of dirt in front of the draft hole.

A hinged or slide door (depending upon the contracting metalsmith's whim) was provided for admitting fuel. This door was eight inches high, six inches wide and eighteen inches from the bottom. The stovepipe connected to the top of the stove consisted of five sections, tapering down from five to four inches. The entire unit was placed beneath the tripod supporting the tent, with a chain and hook suspended from the fork of the tripod on which a kettle could be hung.

The stove weighed twenty-nine or thirty pounds; patent data discloses that there were specifications for a twenty-five- and also an eighteen-pound model but I have never seen an example of the twenty-five pounder. As a matter of fact, I doubt very much that such a model was ever produced. Seems to me there would be little or no reason to have two models so closely akin in size and weight. Possibly Sibley drew up the specifications for both a thirty and a twenty-five pounder and left it up to the Quartermaster General to adopt the one considered to be most advantageous.

But there was an eighteen-pound model. I've seen only two of them during quite a long spell of relicking so these must be regarded as gems—exceedingly rare.

During the course of the Civil War, about 16,000 Sibley stoves were delivered to the U. S. Quartermaster Department for issue to organizations in the field. This certainly isn't a very large inventory in comparison with

Sibleys have undoubtedly contributed measurably to their present scarcity. There was simply nothing about the design of this military-frontier relic to induce preservation by those who have come upon them in the one hundred years since their introduction.

40. *This standard model or thirty-pound Sibley stove is equipped with a shelf attachment and has seen extensive use. Note the repairs made on the base by an Army blacksmith many years ago.*

the hundreds of thousands of rifles, pistols, saddles, sabers and various other items of equipment that were supplied. However, it must be remembered that the original 1857 model Sibley stoves were not products of machine manufacture. Rather, they were hand-fashioned by metalsmiths in foundries and shops with little or no mechanization to speed production.

The unattractive, nondescript characteristics of the

41. *A fine example of the exceedingly scarce eighteen-pound Sibley stove. These were intended for officers' quarters and afforded their users the luxury of a latch device on the firedoor —a feature omitted on most of the thirty-pound models.*

42. *Comparative proportions are evident in the thirty- and eighteen-pound Sibley stoves shown here with open firedoors.*

A good friend of mine who probes around old battlefield and fort sites unearthed one a couple of years ago, but it was so mashed and deteriorated it was beyond restoration.

This brings up the subject of restoring. There's an overzealous tendency on the part of many collectors to rehabilitate relics of this sort by tackling them with ex-tremely harsh abrasives, files and even electric powered emery wheels. Their aggressive effort to clean and freshen up the time-worn surfaces destroys the charm and character of the piece by stripping it of all those little effects of exposure and age which contribute dramatically to the historical aspects of the relic.

I'm not suggesting that lighter rust flakes shouldn't be

removed or that a bad dent shouldn't be carefully tapped out. But the violent application of machinery and strong acids are a senseless approach to proper restoration and have probably done more to ruin a lot of fine frontier antiques than border uprisings or renegade attacks.

A rancher in West Texas recently found a right nice old Sibley stove with a couple of bullet holes in it and a rather beat up stovepipe collar. My boss' son secured the stove by swapping and we wouldn't think of plugging up those terrific old bullet holes. That's what gives the relic a valid claim to having participated in an episode of frontier history. To patch or obliterate those holes would be to make mute the wonderful story it has to tell. We *do*, however, intend to straighten out the roughed up collar. The point here is that restoration is in order but not to the extent of snuffing out the life and soul of the thing.

But back to the old Dragoon. Henry Hopkins Sibley died at Fredericksburg, Virginia, on August 23, 1886. His tent and stove creations had netted him very meager recompense because, when he resigned from the regular U. S. service in 1861 to accept a commission in the Confederate States Army, the Government refused to pay him royalty fees on his patents.

Major Sibley had originally entered into an agreement with the War Department to receive a $5 royalty on each Sibley tent unit supplied to the Army. At $5 per unit, this would have amounted to a pretty sizable head of lettuce, but Uncle Sam consistently disallowed the claims and petitions of the officer and his heirs in the years following the War. Sibley's status as a regular U. S. Army officer had been nullified by his alliance with the Lost Cause.

So today, he is chiefly remembered for that intriguing little sheet iron wrap-around known as the Sibley stove—a distinctively American thing which all collectors of Civil War and Frontier Americana can appreciate.

The collector will have to look before he leaps, though, because there are Sibley-type stoves which were fabricated during a much later period and, therefore, do not qualify as frontier models. They're of identical shape and weight as the earlier ones but principally of machine manufacture. Many are of welded construction and all of them are completely devoid of the hand-riveting and blacksmith-forged characteristics that are evident on the 1857 models. These later ones were issued for use in the CCC camps during the 1930s, and the U. S. Forestry Service had a good many of them in federal parks and game preserves. Although these are a take-off on Old Sibley's design, they aren't the real McCoy, insofar as the knowledgeable collector is concerned, and should be regarded as what they are—great-grandkids of the original 16,000.

Also, there's a semi-circular gizmo, that sometimes is found attached to an old Sibley, which was intended for use as a sort of shelf or tray. Nothing in the Sibley patent data sheds light on the origin of this thing, so it's assumed that troopers, with the cooperative efforts of the camp blacksmith, exercised their soldierly ingenuity in adding this accessory. An adaptation of this kind isn't surprising, as fellers who had to use military equipment in the field frequently altered or re-rigged things in order to provide for better utilization or increased efficiency. These shelves or trays are distinctive little frontier relics in their own right, so if one appears on an old Sibley, it should enhance the value of the stove to the tune of five extra bucks, I would say.

I've got a rather nice twenty-nine pounder that showed up in the Big Hole area of Montana some time ago. Glancing at an old map, I find there were a couple of early forts out that way. The fact that it was recovered in Montana is significant in establishing its relation to the postwar military campaigns against the hostile tribes and gives it the hallmark of a true frontier relic. No doubt my lil' ole Sibley stove shared a tent with some mighty fine young troopers.

The standard 1857 model, if in good shape, is worth $90 to $100. By "good shape," I mean with the Firedoor

43. Two fine examples of Civil War issue kepis. Securing one complete with regimental insignia, buttons and chin strap is an exceptionally hard task.

assembly and stovepipe collar intact and not too heavily rust-pitted or dented. The eighteen pounder is one of those very few items of Frontier Americana which bears a scarcity index of "exceedingly rare." If your hair is **parted just right, $175 to $200 might possibly do the trick.**

KEPI CAP

THOUSANDS OF EX-SOLDIERS headed for western homestead lands immediately following the Civil War. In their wagons were many items of military equipment—army surplus I suppose you'd call it. Anyway, it almost appeared as though the corps were off on another campaign with all the weapons, cavalry hoss gear, camp furnishings and motley assortments of uniform apparel crammed in the wagon boxes of those postwar adventurers.

A not uncommon sight in prairie country during the late '60s was the kepi, or forage cap as it's occasionally called. Stetsons and other wide-brimmed hats just weren't readily available to the struggling sodbuster. Frequently he wore his kepi for the first season or two until the initial crop yielded the price of new headgear.

Old forage caps pop up from time to time at rummage sales and in thrift shops throughout the Midwest. They aren't plentiful. As a matter of fact, they're well-nigh impossible to find in the far West. In the Southwest, that hot sun had a lot to do with their nonacceptance which results in a general unavailability in that region. But in homestead territory (Kansas, Nebraska and thereabouts), a fair number were stashed in trunks and wardrobe cabinets throughout the rural communities and that's where most of them are lurking today.

Whenever descendents of the original settlers go to dividing up the estate by auctions and gifts to organizations employing the handicapped, some of these tattered remnants of the homestead era come to light. Here's where the Civil War buffs get into the picture again. They have bid these relics up until they've become just about the scarcest of all leather and fabric accessories associated with sodbuster life and times.

I don't suppose one could hope to secure a kepi now for less than $20 to $25 and this pricing doesn't reflect a consideration for good condition. Most of the kepis I've seen have had moth holes in the woolen crown and cracked, brittle edges on the visors. Regimental insignia is usually missing and the little buttons that held the strap in place are frequently crushed or missing. Union buttons and insignia can be replaced at a modest cost because dealers have obtained portions of the sizable inventory of these items that were stored in government warehouses at the close of the War. Confederate material along this line is practically nonexistent. It'll be mighty tough to find a kepi in tip-top shape, so $30 for a not-too-shoddy one is about the best a guy can hope for. One in superb condition, if such there be, should be easily worth twice that price.

ODDMENTS OF FORT AND TRAIL

THIS MAY SOUND rather strange, but the year 1946 opened up an entirely new era in the lore of Frontier Americana. For almost a century, relics and fragments of the Old West in countless thousands had been hidden, from a few inches to a foot or so, beneath the crumbling ruins of old forts and camp sites, battlefields, deserted towns and outposts.

For many years, telephone people have utilized metal detectors and various sensitive devices as a means of locating underground lines and cables. Army Ordnance developed mine detecting instruments that were quite effective and paid off big dividends during the war years. With the termination of World War II, these devices with advanced electronic components were made generally available to the public. Treasure hunters and relickers lost little time securing them for use in the recovery and preservation of the many items of historical value that had been undisturbed for decades beneath the shifting topsoil of western settlements.

The photographs shown here depict quite well the type of thing Mother Earth yields to the frequency pitches of those detecting devices. Each and every one of the intensely interesting objects on these display plaques has a colorful and dramatic story to tell. In many respects, these intriguing old relics, artifacts and fragments relate chapters in frontier history that are closer to the core of the actual deeds than the cold words of written accounts will ever come. Here is the tangible evidence of the toil, struggle, courage, hopes and dreams, suffering and privation, and rugged, bold determination of the Westerner in his search for a better life for himself and his family.

Value? I ought to defer any attempt to evaluate the worth of these wonderful objects in a purely monetary sense. It's fairly easy to arrive at a trade value for a Sibley stove, a branding iron or an eighteen-inch specimen of early barbed wire. But what's an old, rusty picket pin or an empty cartridge case worth?

Not long ago I chatted with an antique dealer concerning the criteria by which a lot of old, rusted, broken and deteriorated fragments should be appraised in order to

44. Mounted in a novel and fascinating manner are relics of the old Santa Fe Trail. The Colt Navy revolver was found near Pawnee Rock, Kansas, a famous Indian vantage point on the Trail. Arrowheads, tomahawk, oxshoe, hider's knife and bullets illustrate the story of emigrant hardships on the trek westward. Anyone with imagination can fix up a similar display for den or trophy room.

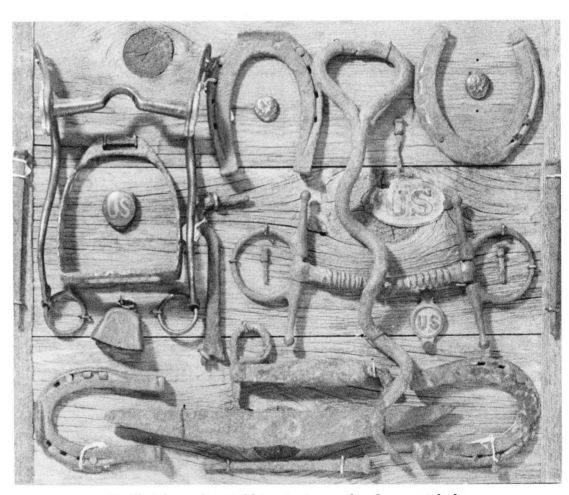

45. All of these relics of old frontier forts and trails were picked up around the crumbling ruins of early settlements and campsites along the Butterfield Trail.

arrive at something resembling realistic pricing. He remarked that "The stuff is worth whatever a body is willing to pay for it."

I can't entirely agree with either his philosophical or business approach to this matter—nor can I find much of a basis for disagreement. There is hardly a relic mounted on these display panels worth more than a couple of dollars, with the exception of that old Colt Navy revolver and the military stirrup which, also, has something of an established market value. But for the most part, these old oddments of iron and brass do not clamor for recognition through means of a fixed worth in dollars and cents. Their value lies chiefly in what they convey to us, in a literal sort of way, about the lives and times of the courageous men who forged and used them. Something like a good book valued at a couple of dollars, between the covers of which is a fascinating story. Yes—something like the price of a good book!

TABLE OF VALUES

The column on the right denotes the degree of scarcity of each relic. The numbers assign a scarcity factor as follows: 1–3 common, 4–6 scarce, 7–9 rare.

Relic	Fair	Good	Excellent	Scarcity Factor
Kepi or Forage Cap				
Confederate	$25	$ 40+	$ 60	7
Union	$20	$ 30	$ 40+	6
Oddments of Fort and Trail	Unpriced—See the text			
Sibley Stove (1857)				
18 Pounder	$85	$150	$175–200	9
29–30 Pounder	$50	$ 80	$100	6

AT THE BUNKHOUSE

46. "Cutting Out" is another in the remarkable series of western paintings done by 22-year-old N. C. Wyeth in the early summer of 1904. Here he has depicted, with exceptional vigor the wild, spectacular excitement that was all part of a day's work on the open range.

TIDY RACK

ABOUT NINETY-EIGHT per cent of the furniture and household furnishings hauled westward during emigrant days cannot be classified as western in the truest sense of the word.

For the most part the equipment and furniture used in homesteads, lodging houses and residences on the frontier had a rather cosmopolitan background. Much of it was what we call early- and mid-Victorian. Much more of it had a simple, plain—even austere—quality; it was the type furniture many antiquers insist upon calling Colonial, Primitive, or Early American. At any rate, the bulk of the stuff was of a universal character and cannot be appropriately designated as essentially western.

There are a couple of peculiar little articles of cabinetmaking, nevertheless, that do clamor for attention and recognition as distinctly frontier-type furnishings. One is called a tidy rack (a rather goofy name, I think); another is a certain type of pie safe. Here we're concerned with the tidy rack, so let's take a look at the one I found a couple of years ago in an old abandoned bunkhouse in West Texas.

It was mounted shoulder high on the slab wall over a spot where a washstand had once stood. Its purpose is quite apparent for it is nothing more than an encased mirror, with a comb tray and a couple of rings for holding huckaback towels.

When I first found this rather undignified wall accessory, I hadn't the foggiest idea as to its origin. After a little research into general store inventories and through conversations with some elderly midwestern folks, I learned that these tidy racks were crafted principally for the western market and were used quite extensively in bunkhouses, washup sheds that adjoined soddy kitchens, and at remote line camp cabins. The measurements of the one I have provide a good bit in the way of conveying the overall heft of the thing: nineteen inches high, about eleven inches wide and—get this—five-eighths of an inch thick. It weighs pretty close to four pounds—solid oak! A good safe measure in fastening the thing to the wall over the washstand was to spike it there. It's these characteristics of bulk, weight and durability that stamp it as a product intended for frontier use. Obviously it was made to take a lot of hard knocks. The peddler who could have hawked these bold, graceless accessories back East would surely have been a "huckster *par excellénce.*"

Tidy racks aren't overly scarce—nor common, either. I've seen possibly a half-dozen during the past few years—one real nice one in an antique shop. That's where I found out what they were called. The lady shopkeeper commented casually, "You really should buy that tidy rack, Sir. It's the only one I've found during my last

47. Found in an abandoned bunkhouse, this tidy rack is typical of wall accessories that were crafted principally for the western market. Huckaback towels hung from the stout wooden rings below the comb tray.

two buying trips." I must agree with her observation that they're more "elusive" than might be supposed. But here I would say that this scarcity factor is a deceptive element because tidy racks were articles of machine manu-facture and that, in itself, gives a sort of volume back-ground to the relic. I'll wager that many have been pitched into attics and storage sheds throughout the Midwest, Southwest and far West. Therefore, I won't go so far as to say they're ultrascarce. The term "elusive" still seems to me to be the most descriptive.

The one in the antique shop was tagged $18, and was perhaps a bit underpriced. I rather imagine this modest charge was largely the result of the unsophisticated proportions of the piece—a condition that always detracts from the value of a relic in relation to its essential worth from a scarcity point of view. So $20 to $24 is dirt cheap for a tidy rack because this is just another item that hasn't yet been fully accepted as significant to the lore of the frontier. If you're a weekend relic hunter and you come upon one lying inconspicuously in the corner of an abandoned farmhouse, latch onto it pronto! You've found yourself one of the few articles of Frontier Americana that might well be termed a sleeper.

BOOTJACKS

IF A FELLER happens to know the whereabouts of an old abandoned ranch house or cowboy hangout, there's a downright strong possibility he could snoop around the place for awhile and come up with an old bootjack. Probably not the fancy cast iron or brass jobs (the store-bought variety), but the more common, homemade, wooden "V" notch kind. Old bootjacks are still knocking around the West in considerable numbers so it's merely a matter of diggin' them out.

About three or four designs may be considered typically frontier types. It seems as if westerners had a preference for certain ones like Naughty Lady, the Bulldog Pistol 'jack, the Cricket and the Beetle. Another one, a

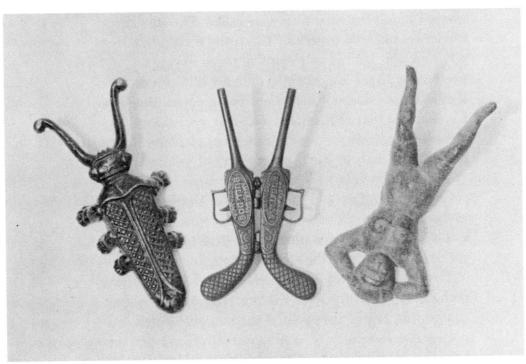

48. *At left is the popular Beetle bootjack. The Bulldog, center, folds up to resemble a pistol. Naughty Nellie, at right, was a perennial bunkhouse favorite. All of these examples are cast iron; however, most foundries also produced them in brass.*

49. Homemade bootjacks are still to be found in and about many rangeland communities. They're desirable as a primitive form in contrast to the novel, ornate bootjacks of brass and iron that were sold at general stores throughout the West.

sort of lyre-shaped pattern, acquired only a limited patronage.

The Naughty Lady (marketed also as Naughty Nellie) was a real bunkhouse favorite, and is pretty hard to find these days. There's a good, sound reason why. Homemakers of a later era, in carrying out home decoration schemes, got to using old bootjacks as doorstops. A good deal of partiality was shown toward the amusing Cricket and Beetle; but, Naughty Nellie was considered by genteel housewives as a mite indiscreet. As a result of that extremely prejudiced opinion, many of these fine bootjacks suffered a trash pile fate and, consequently, are nudging the scarce bracket.

Wooden "V" notch bootjacks, rustic and strictly utilitarian in nature, are the easiest to find. They're quite desirable as a form of frontier primitive. The old square nail joinery gives them a homespun charm which is really pleasing in spite of their overall lack of decorative pattern. When found at country auctions or in junk shops, they usually can be had for a few dollars—$8 to $10 at most for an especially nice one.

The Beetles and Crickets, in cast iron or brass, go for something like $15 to $18, demonstrating an unusual market condition. Normally castings of brass are priced considerably higher than iron because of manufacturers' production expense in using the more costly metal. Most dealers price the metals alike which violates that rule. Justification is probably based on the simple fact that there are more brass than iron bootjacks generally available.

To secure a brass Naughty Nellie, the collector ought to figure on coughing up at least $25. The lyre-shaped bootjack, although peddled to some extent in the West, has always appeared to me as sorter eastern lookin'—a little bit Duncan Phyfe in style and character. Guess it's deserving of display in a western grouping, however, and I'd go $12 for one—no more. The Bulldog Pistol is a humdinger of a decorator and this feature alone moves it into a desirable category. I don't feel $25, even $28, is too dear for one!

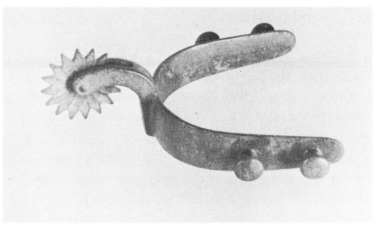

51. *The famous OK spur was exceptionally popular with working cowhands. Its practical design was adaptable to the general conditions of everyday range life.*

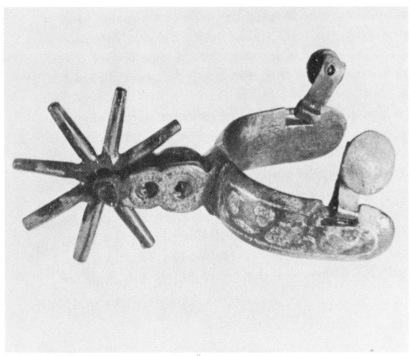

50. *The Chihuahua spur is closely identified with the* vaqueros *and riders of the southwestern border country. This example is plain as compared to other very ornately crafted ones. The huge rowel and the gold and silver inlay are characteristics of Spanish-type spurs.*

SPURS

IF YOU WERE to have poked your head inside the doorway of an old bunkhouse, chances are you'd have seen four or five cowhands lounging around with four or five different types of spurs on their boots. There were just about as many different styles of spurs as there were riders in the Old West so it's nigh-on to impossible to cover more than a few typical ones that the collector may encounter. Since spur designs range from the simplest spiked projections to ultrafancy gold and silver inlay specimens, the ones cited here will serve as a representative group of those types chiefly identified with western rangelands. A cavalry spur is tossed in for good measure.

First is the Chihuahua, a *vaquero*- or Mexican-styled spur, characterized by three prominent features: heaviness, ornateness and a jumbo-sized rowel (usually three or four inches in diameter). Many Chihuahua spurs are decorated with silver and/or gold inlay and, surprisingly, were originally sold for considerably less than their American-made counterparts.

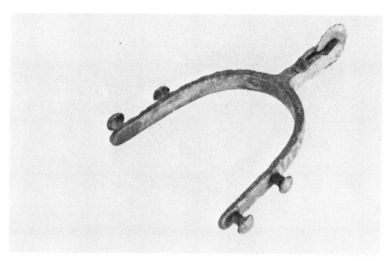

52. This old spur with sawtooth rowel was found in a trash heap near Austin, Texas. It appears to be much more appropriate for a gentleman rider than for cowboys with half-wild mustangs.

Throughout the entire southwestern border country this style spur seems to have played a major role. They're not too hard to find and, notwithstanding their age (seventy or eighty years, maybe), still bring a price little in excess of their original cost. Western literature hasn't always given the *vaqueros* a fair shake in citing their numerical proportions relative to the other fellers who made up the crews of our western cow camps. There surely must have been a bunch of *vaqueros* riding the border rangelands if these Chihuahua spurs are any indication. There are a lot of 'em around.

Quite a favorite of the American cowhand was the famous OK spur first introduced in the early '80s. Most of the old-time cowboys still around today have a great deal of nostalgic respect for this fine spur because, in many

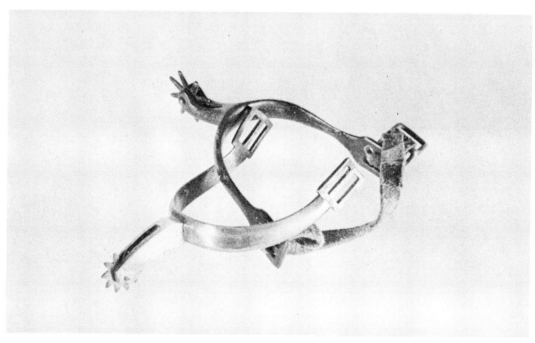

53. Cavalry spurs of the Custer era. The brass one in the foreground is an officer's issue. An enlisted trooper wore the iron spur which still has a portion of the original strap attached.

instances, this was the one they first broke out with. The high arch of its shank is probably the only thing that might be considered a little unusual in comparison with other general utility spurs.

About a year ago I found an old spur at a dump. By the way, I'm not in the least adverse to probing around old trash heaps and I hope you're not either. That's where some of my most cherished "junque" has come from. Anyway, I picked up an old straight shanked spur with a sawtooth rowel, rather different from a lot of western spurs in one respect. The little sawtooth rowel is of the type that is usually found on dress spurs—purely an ornamental wheel not intended to serve much as a goading device. The rest of the spur is rugged, crudely crafted and obviously meant to do a job for a working cowhand. So here we have a spur that seems torn between devotion and duty. It can't decide between being dressy or worth its salt as a real cowboy spur. According to what I've read, it never achieved any measurable degree of popularity and I can't say that it deserved much.

Custer-era cavalry spurs, of brass or fine tempered metal, are the very essence of usefulness. A bit austere, they possess a sort of simple elegance that reflects a trim military bearing combined with the capacity to provide a limited goading effect. Cavalry mounts were pretty well-trained and needed a minimum of such treatment so the spur seems to suit the conditions quite well. They're getting scarce and are especially tough to find in pairs. This never ceases to worry me because most cowboy spurs seem to show up in pairs—like old bunkmates. Cavalry spurs, however, have a high AWOL rate that's hard to explain. Kinda late now, I suppose, but the military ought to look into this.

Here we go on prices again. A pair of Chihuahuas are worth $12 to $14. The OK spurs are a buy at the same price, maybe $15, tops. The offbeat straight shank spur with the sawtooth rowel is worth $5 or $6 and the cavalry spurs wouldn't be overpriced at $15 a pair. Don't confuse these older cavalry spurs with the later ones (steel mostly) which have been about in some quantity since the disbanding of several cavalry units prior to World War II.

STEER SKULL

THERE'S REALLY NOTHING earthshaking about an old range steer's skull except that one will make a den wall look downright western and the market value is so depressed, cost will be negligible—seldom more than a few dollars.

This relic is not nearly as difficult to find as a buffalo skull. I found one lying along the shoulder of an old country road a few months back. My wife hates the thing. She says it's macabre and hideous. Maybe that's because I had the old rascal hung up in the spare bedroom for a spell. I wanted to make a close study of its proportions and details in connection with some illustrations I was shaping up. At any rate, an old steer skull is a sort of western trademark—a symbol of the days when the cattle empires were among the most dominant elements in the expansion and development of the vast frontier. The skull I found exemplifies much of that colorful era—that bygone range. It has character and I like it. (Incidentally, it hangs out in the garage now.)

What's been referred to above is, of course, an ordinary, run-of-the-mill steer skull. A tremendous old longhorn skull with an impressive horn span of four or five feet is an entirely different matter and the market is far from depressed on this kind of relic. Can't say that I've seen more than two or three of them outside of museums during the past several years—the *complete* skull with horns, that is. This is undoubtedly because folks considered those tremendous horns as the sole trophy and got to collecting them aside from the big passel o' bone that

54. *The irregularity of mismatched horns gives this old range steer's skull a weird appearance. He's a symbol of the open range and contributes dramatically toward decorative effect in a display of things western.*

grew 'em. So a skull sproutin' its original longhorns will be about as tough to run down as a chuck wagon box.

Throughout the West, particularly at trading posts and tourist centers you'll find highly polished longhorns sweeping out of a tooled leather sleeve. The leathercraft is little more than a stylized hunk of something where the old skull ought to be. These are interesting, I suppose, and do bear a somewhat remote identification with the old critter himself. However, they shouldn't be regarded as anything more than nostalgic novelties without the primitive, wild character that is so excitingly evident in an old skull and horns left intact.

From what I've been able to learn about these novelty horns, they come in two distinct forms: one is a right superb grade of plastic molded and figured to such a degree of realism that a feller could be quite easily fooled into thinking it is the real thing; the other is a set of true longhorns brought in from Mexico where a couple of fair-sized herds of descendents of the original critters are kept in game preserves for lease to movie people. Occasionally, a fine old rascal is sold off as a zoo specimen or mascot.

Even though I've kept an eye open for an authentic longhorn skull for quite some time now, they're few and far between and it may very well be that the one in the garage is about as close as I'll ever come to locating an old knave of the open range. The thrill is in the hunt, however, and, until the real one comes along, the one I have will do. Hate to think of what the better half will say, though, if I should find "Ole Pancho" someday!

TABLE OF VALUES

The column on the right denotes the degree of scarcity of each relic. The numbers assign a scarcity factor as follows: 1–3 common, 4–6 scarce, 7–9 rare.

Relic	Fair	Good	Excellent	Scarcity Factor
Bootjacks				
Cast Iron:				
Beetle, Cricket	$10	$14	$18	3
Bulldog Pistol	$15	$20	$25+	5
Naughty Nellie	$12	$16	$22.50+	5
Naughtie Nellie (brass)	$15	$22.50	$27.50	5
Others:				
Lyre-Shaped	$ 7	$ 9	$12–15	4
Wood "V" Notch	$ 5	$ 7.50	$10	2
Spurs (Pairs)				
Cavalry Officers or Enlisted Troopers	$ 7	$12.50	$17.50	5
Chihuahua	$ 6	$ 9	$12–14	5
Miscellaneous	$ 5	$ 6	$ 8	2
OK	$ 7	$10	$14	4
Steer Skull				
Longhorn Steer	$30	$45	$75+	7
Ordinary Range Steer	$ 6	$10	$15	2
Tidy Rack	$12	$18	$25+	5

AT THE HIDE HUNTER'S CAMP

55. *"Indian Trapper" by the distinguished western illustrator, Frederic Remington.*

BUFFALO SKULL

56. "White Trapper" by the distinguished western illustrator, Frederic Remington. This remarkable painting depicts well the rugged individualism, courage and adventurous spirit of the frontier "loner"—the mountain man.

IF SOMEONE WERE to ask me to cite a single relic which symbolizes or best represents the color and very spirit of the Old West, I'd surely have to hesitate a spell before replying. So many significant things immediately come to

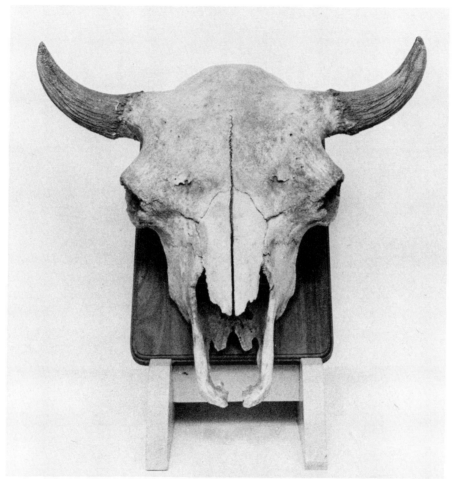

57. Picked up on the Kansas prairie, this old buffalo skull is a constant reminder of the vast herds that once roamed the West. It is in remarkably fine condition, with the lower skeletal structure almost entirely intact.

mind—the Conestoga wagon, the old plainsman's rifle, the fringed buckskins of the mountain man, perhaps a branding iron or an old muleshoe—I don't know.

Then I look across the room and absorb, for a minute or two, the tremendous power and drama which Charles M. Russell's skill has created in the beautiful western painting that hangs there. My eye wanders to a lower

corner of that masterpiece and a little monogram inscribed near the edge of the frame tells a story which embraces something extremely poignant in the western panorama. It tells a tale that's bold and powerful—and sad. Modestly placed beneath C. M. Russell's signature is the small, sketchy outline of a buffalo skull. Charlie's symbol, I believe, is as close to the pulse of the Old West as one could ever hope to come.

The old bull skull on the wall of my den had long been buried beneath a sand bar on the Smoky Hill River in central Kansas. It came to light some fifteen years ago and has changed hands a few times since. Although it's not a complete skull, there wasn't much quibbling when I bargained for it because they're hard to find in any condition these days. The trophy value of these relics was recognized 'way back in the 1870s and those that were preserved are quite protectively regarded by the present-day descendents of their original owners. The jawbones on mine are missing but the bony horn protuberances are still intact and that's sufficient to give it enough character to be identified as an old "buffler."

After the heyday of the hide hunters, prairie bone pickers did away with hundreds of thousands of weathered, sun-bleached buffalo skulls which were marketed for conversion into fertilizer. There are not too many old bison skulls around and of those that have survived, completeness of the specimen will just about be the only basis for determining value.

One with the horns undamaged, with the eyesockets and lower jaw skeletal structure complete, must be reguarded as a premium specimen worth around $65 to $75. Skulls with serious defects such as broken horns or shattered jawbones are worth considerably less. As a happy medium, I'd say $30 to $40 is a fair price to pay for a not-too-beat-up old buffalo skull. Of course, a massive bull skull should be worth more than the smaller cow skull, condition factors being equal.

These true frontier relics make fascinating centerpieces for western displays. Any buffalo skull, whether it be a trophy from the prairie herds of a hundred years ago or one from their government-protected offspring, is a mighty desirable addition to a collection.

I had an eye peeled for the one in my den for a couple of years before he tagged on home with me. Somewhere along the old Smoky Hill River there's probably a little more of him buried deep in that sand bar. Even if I knew where it was, I wouldn't care to disturb it now.

HIDE HUNTER'S KNIFE

I'M AWFULLY DUBIOUS about assigning a definite nomenclature to the hide hunter's skinning knife. It would be misleading to say that the hider used a certain, specialized type of blade—one that was specifically designed for skinning purposes. True, the famous Green River knife didn't suffer for lack of patronage. However, during the era when those codgers were peppering away at nearly everything that moved, there simply wasn't an overly fussy attitude about what kind of a skinning knife was right or proper—just so it was sharp and durable!

In museum displays throughout the West, I've seen a dozen or more types, each of which was tagged as an authentic "hider's knife." These relics run the entire gamut from ordinary butchers' blades to fancy-handled daggers. A few were Bowie knives.

Perhaps the most surprising discovery was the high proportion of homemade blades utilized by those crafty gents. Some were nothing more than blacksmith files that had been sharpened and fitted into rude grips or handles. I saw one fashioned from the broken blade of a carpenter's drawknife. Consequently, it's nigh-on to impossible to classify a hider's knife as a specific form. Anything that took on the appearance of a stout blade was used to skin the slain beasts of forest and prairie.

Of the three typical knives illustrated here, two are of an improvised nature and the other "store bought"—of the Green River variety. Since this Green River product seems to pop up quite often in the lore of the Old West, it's appropriate to remark briefly concerning the quality edges those folks put out.

58. *A blade of superior quality, the famous Green River knife was used by frontiersmen, trappers and hunters throughout the West. This one was found along the Santa Fe Trail.*

Prior to 1836, the cutlery market in this country was dominated by imports from the famous shops in Sheffield and Birmingham, England. It didn't take long for Yankee ingenuity to assert itself, however. A silversmith named John Russell got busy and set up shop at a site on Green River near Deerfield, Massachusetts. He developed some labor-saving machinery which, together with quality materials and skilled hands, turned out a line of knives that were able to stand the gaff, both in serviceability and competitively. The John Russell Company produced table knives, butcher and carving knives, and pocket and hunting knives—in fact, every type of edged blade conceivable.

Many of these excellent edges found their way into hide hunters' sheaths and kits to be employed as tools of the trade. Most of these blades are stamped "J. Russell & Co., Green River Works" above a small diamond-shaped trade symbol—hence, the name "Green River Knife." The most popular one was a slightly curved blade about six inches long with a plain wooden handle fastened by brass rivets. Nothing very distinctive or attractive about it— just a good quality blade meant to be used where hefty knife-wielding was required.

Although the individually crafted ones were no more serviceable or advantageous (in many cases they were less practical than the manufactured ones), there's a great deal more uniqueness to their shape and make-up. This must be said of most all relics that were hand-fashioned. They're definitely not "peas in a pod."

The old buffalo horn handle on the one shown is a tremendous example of the "personal" touch. It was found in the Midwest by a friend of mine among the effects of a long-gone hide hunter. It had been stashed in his saddle bag. The other is one I picked up at a rummage sale a few years ago. It, too, is entirely homespun, having been fashioned from an ordinary file. The rasp surface is still evident along the edges encased by the oak handle.

All of these knives—the Green River, the horn-handle and the file blade—are typical of that essential item of the hide hunter's gear—his skinning tool. In analyzing them again, I'm more certain than ever that there's no such thing as an approved, specific, standard or other-

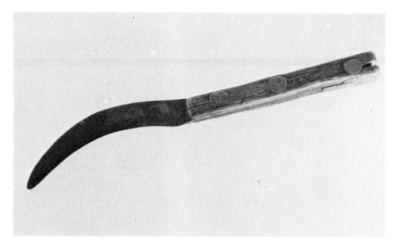

60. A surprisingly high percentage of old skinning knives were individually crafted by the hiders themselves from discarded tools and edges. This one was made from a worn out blacksmith's file.

59. This skinning knife was found among the effects of an old hide hunter. The buffalo horn handle is truly unique and endows the relic with a distinctively western character.

wise specialized type. They seem to be about as individual and nonconforming as the men who used them. The price range applicable to them must necessarily be correspondingly flexible.

With such diversity of substance, it's difficult to nail it down tight, but a good old hider's blade should be worth from $20 to $35 with uniqueness or "character" being a strong guideline when judging value. Oh yes—one more thing. They're getting downright scarce!

BEAVER TRAP

MOST HIDE HUNTERS were specialists, after a fashion. The beaver men plied their trade along the swift rivers and streams that coursed through wild, heavily forested regions of the far West. Others went after the prime pelts that were taken up high near the timberline. These men were a distinct breed—loners, mostly! Occasionally, two would team up for mutual advantage if each had a certain know-how that the other lacked.

They were dyed-in-the-wool adventurers—those mountain men and frontier trappers—true sportsmen. So long as a trapper baited his steel-jawed trap upon which a telltale human scent adhered, the animal had a choice—take the bait or leave it alone. There was seldom, even in the dead of winter, a critical scarcity of fare in the wilderness. Theirs was a way of life in which the wits of man were matched against the cunning and instinct of the beast—a fair and decent manner for one to glean his sustenance from the pantry of Mother Nature.

Buffalo hunters were of an entirely different species. They frequently banded together with a kind of industrial organization set-up. There were shooters, skinners, stakers, cooks, caravan tenders and so forth—all functioning in a methodical pattern of killing, skinning, curing, loading and killing again. It was strictly cold critter to cold cash. That's why I have a particular affection for a trap. It represents the fair means by which mountain men, trappers and frontiersmen turned an honest buck.

Since we've afforded space in the display cabinet to accommodate hide hunters' knives, a shaggy jacket, the Sharps rifle and what's left of a monarch of the prairie, it's more than fitting that a beaver trap be placed in the cabinet, also.

Old traps aren't too hard to come by. Even though these relics are to be associated with those early days when the only white men west of the Mississippi were trappers and traders, the fact remains that every sodbuster, rancher and farmer had traps for wolves, coyotes, skunks and varmints of similar ilk. It shouldn't be too difficult to pick up an old trap for $7.50 to $12.

Not a bear trap, mind you! Old "bar" traps are scarce and the junkmen know it. They bring from $35 to $75 chiefly because their enormous size has put them into a certain category which the trade butters up as conversation pieces. Personally, I prefer to "converse" with smaller stuff and that's not because of any animosity toward "bar" traps. It's simply that my den is small and it puts a terrible crick in my neck when I try to commune with relics displayed on the ceiling!

SHAGGY JACKET

THROUGHOUT THE FAR West (particularly the Northwest), fringed buckskin jackets and leggings which were worn by frontiersmen and Indians alike pop up from time

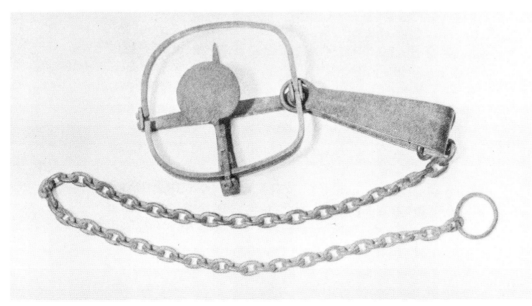

61. A beaver trap of the type used on the frontier more than a century ago. This one, without jagged teeth, has a maker's mark—"B. Sanderson"—location unknown. It has a jaw spread of eight inches.

to time when old trunks are auctioned off or otherwise disposed of in remote communities. A "shaggy" or buffalo hide jacket makes an appearance even less frequently. They are strange articles of apparel—"oddball" to use a more contemporary term—and they rate a position somewhere between fairly and exceedingly scarce because of a couple of circumstances.

First, undisciplined curing methods employed by roving trappers and hide hunters certainly didn't contribute much toward insuring a high measure of permanence to the hair surface. The nonprofessional tanning procedures were such as to cause the hair to part company with the hide after a few seasons. Most of these homemade jackets just didn't withstand the ravages of time.

Second, the dad-burned things were inclined to be smelly for quite a spell. This wasn't so noticeable in open country, but the garments became mighty pungent when stored for any length of time. This ripeness prompted disposal by inheritors who were just a trifle sensitive to the fragrance of things wild.

The one pictured here was included with the inventory of a large gun and Indian artifact collection that was consigned to an Ohio doctor many years ago. Maybe it was part of his fee for "patch-up" and sundry comforts rendered. I dunno about that, but the dealer who later acquired and offered it for $35 had priced it fairly. The fact that this jacket is in tolerably good shape and doesn't smell too badly is a belated tribute to the feller who made it more than eighty years ago. One could hardly class this relic as a magnificent example of Frontier Americana, but it certainly is something different. How many "shaggy" jackets have you seen knocking around used clothing stores lately?

62. *This waist length buffalo skin jacket, made by an old hider for wear astride his mount, is an unusual and rather scarce relic. Though somewhat clumsy in appearance, the full cut sleeves and shoulders afforded the rifleman adequate freedom of motion.*

HIDERS' SCALES

THE COLLECTOR OF Frontier Americana will probably, at one time or another, come upon a relic or accessory that possesses an authentic western heritage, but the "why-for" of the thing will be puzzling. The scales shown here afford a good case in point. I know they're bona fide western scales since I found them a few years ago in the debris of a caved-in prairie dugout along with a beat-up skinning blade, some rusty traps, and a heap of rotten furs (which I shore didn't molest!). Everything pointed to the fact that this motley assortment of effects once belonged to a hider.

Tension scales of this type were used by soddies, ranchers and farmers for many purposes relative to their particular livelihoods. On a couple of occasions, I've seen these scales displayed with western relics and labeled "trapper's scales." In a Shreveport, Louisiana, collection, there are some tagged "cotton scales." One thing's for certain—they got around. Therefore, these relics can be accepted as authentic items of Frontier Americana on the strength of those associations alone. But what purpose did the scales serve for the hider?

Wal, an evening of probing the reference shelf seemed to be a logical approach toward unraveling this mystery. My book browsings into the lore of the hiders and the procedures involved in their trading practices didn't clarify much on the subject of weights and measures. Hides, pelts, furs, skins—whatever one chooses to call them—were traded by the hunter or trapper on an "each" basis, so far as I can determine. So many dollars for a prime pelt; quality, size and color calling for the giving or taking of a dollar or two one way or the other.

Fur trading was governed, essentially, by the ups and downs of market quotations emanating from eastern trade centers. Bulk weight was definitely a factor among tanners and leather merchants. We can also rule aside the activities of the bone picker since his cargo was marketed by the ton.

So, the inclusion of scales in a hide hunter's gear still amounted to something of an enigma. Unless, of course, the old rascal used them for weighing something other than hides. Like buffalo tongues, for example!

Tongues were in great demand back East—a real

delicacy—and the information I've been able to root out verifies that they were traded and marketed by the pound. This would tend to explain the presence of scales in a hider's kit. Mine are not worth much more than $6 or $8, I reckon, but in view of the fact that there are so few items that can be closely linked to the camp of an old

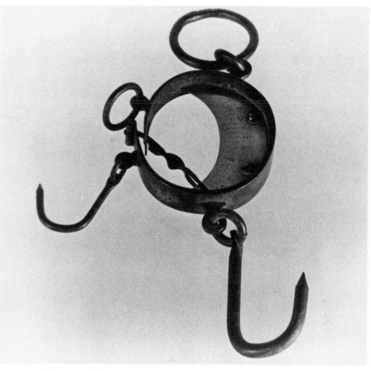

63. Hiders' scales found in an old caved-in prairie dugout. A sack or object suspended from either hook causes the oval frame to spread, thereby moving the indicator upward into the crescent-shaped poundage plate.

hide hunter, these scales deserve a slight nod of recognition.

SHARPS RIFLE

THE BUFFALO HUNTER, the gink who was out there blasting away at the American bison as a professional undertaking, couldn't very well afford to monkey around with a firearm that didn't deliver the goods. His was an enterprise that involved some pretty big game and it didn't take long for him to adopt a weapon that had the Sunday punch he needed—the Sharps rifle.

Christian Sharps had experimented with the old Hall's patent breechloader while he was employed at the Harpers Ferry armory back in the early 1840s. From Hall's system of feeding a charge from the chamber into

Two things it did have, however. First, a skilled shooter could count on sending the .45/90 caliber ball a good 800 to 900 yards with reasonable accuracy. Second, even though it was a single shot rifle, a hunter could get off four shots a minute by virtue of the efficient breechblock reloading mechanism. With its rather short barrel and saddle ring on the side it was adaptable for use on horseback—another advantageous feature the Westerner readily acknowledged.

Two Sharps models saw extensive service on the fron-

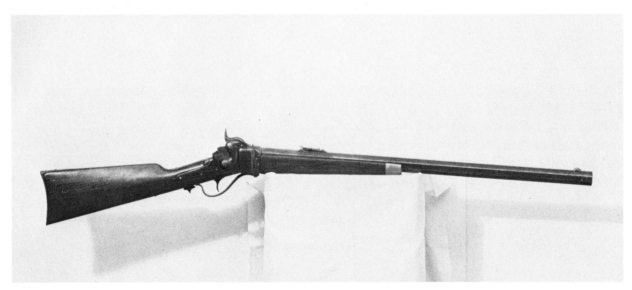

64. The Sharps rifle was the most noted of the guns used on the frontier. With a rather short barrel, it was particularly adaptable for use on horseback. This one used the .45/90 cartridge.

the bore of the weapon, Sharps developed, in 1848, the first successful breechloader. It was successful in that it was a significant improvement over everything previously produced, even though it did have a few operational bugs that were never quite ironed out of it. Gas escaped at the breech where the seam between the chamber and the barrel had not been machined to fit properly, and other parts goofed up with regular frequency due to faulty tolerances.

tier: the regular Sharps with a vertical breech and another, considerably scarce, with a slanting breech. Most buffalo hunters used the vertical breech model, but during the 1850s Sharps' breechloading carbines and rifles were toted by trailmasters, soldiers, Indians and settlers throughout the entire expanse from Missouri to California. This is pretty conclusive testimony that the barrels of these old weapons were puttin' out wisps of smoke where a lot of western history was taking place.

It seems that some of those wisps of smoke are drifting around the antique arms market today. However, they've taken on a different shape. They look like dollar signs— BIG dollar signs. A Sharps slanting breech model will blast a whopping big hole in a $300 pay check. If a collector is in the $150 bracket, the best he can hope for is a regular Sharps model—and go home broke.

Does the Sharps buffalo rifle have a valid claim to fame? Or should it be regarded as having contributed more toward an infamous episode in western history? The idealist will look at it one way, the apologist another, and a practical feller would probably say that if the Sharps hadn't rid the prairies of the American bison, another weapon surely would have. The psychologist ought to get his word in edgewise, too. He'll say, "Don't blame the rifles; blame the men who fired them."

Fame or infamy, it's all part of history now and the old Sharps rifle stands in the gun cabinet looking pretty much as if it didn't give a hoot. I can't say I feel quite that way, though. In all fairness, it's proper to admit that those old rifles brought about a heap of good—while they were taking something away.

There have been times on bleak winter evenings, as I worked alone in my den, when I would stop for a few moments, lay down my crow-quill pen, push aside my work, and look up at my old buffalo bull skull hanging there over the pie safe book cabinet. From 'way off across the prairies I could hear a faint rumble of thunder—the dull pounding of thousands of hoofs. Sometimes my son would walk in, sit down quietly, look at the drawing on the sketch board, and then glance over toward the window.

"Wind's risin' out there again, Dad," he'd say.

TABLE OF VALUES

The column on the right denotes the degree of scarcity of each relic. The numbers assign a scarcity factor as follows: 1–3 common, 4–6 scarce, 7–9 rare.

Relic	Fair	Good	Excellent	Scarcity Factor
Buffalo Skull	$ 30	$ 40+	$ 70+	7
Hider's Scales	$ 4.50	$ 6	$ 8.50	4
Shaggy Jacket	$ 15	$ 27.50	$ 45	5
Sharps Rifle				
Regular Breech	$ 95	$135	$165+	5
Slanting Breech	$185	$250	$300+	8
Skinning Knives				
Green River	$ 15	$ 30+	$ 50+	7
Homemade				
Common	$ 7.50	$ 12	$ 18–20	3
Unique	$ 12	$ 22.50	$ 35	7
Traps				
Bear	$ 25+	$ 45	$ 70+	6
Beaver, Coyote,				
Wolf, etc.	$ 6	$ 8.50	$ 12–15	4

AT THE RANCH HOUSE

65. "*The wild, spectacular race for dinner*" *is another of N. C. Wyeth's superb portrayals of the bold ruggedness so typical of men in the cattle country. Painted in 1904 at Cottonwood Camp, Colorado, when the artist was twenty-two years old.*

BUFFALO BILL STATUETTES

It's PRETTY MUCH a toss up as to whether Buffalo Bill Cody's fame rests more on his exploits as a hunter and scout or on his abilities as a super-showman. The old boy had a mighty good eye for leveling rifle sights on a "buffler"; his peepers were also exceptionally keen when it came to spotting a way to turn an extra buck around the arena. The wild, exciting and colorful panorama of whooping riders and careening stagecoaches has long ago passed into show world limbo but some of the wares of his novelty vendors still survive.

Souvenir programs, tomahawks, peace pipes, pistol watch fobs and figurines were all part of his Wild West Show, and collectors of Frontier Americana can be grateful. The figurines and statuettes, in particular, constitute a limited field of collectables recognized now as a distinct form of western folk art.

The little equestrian statuette of Buffalo Bill shown here is a ten-inch-high, pot metal casting that my grandmother got from an Indian hawker at a performance in Buffalo, New York, sometime around 1895. As a kid, I can recall Granny telling of the thrilling spectacle and of how she sweet-talked my grandpa into buying the little statuette for her. She never forgot to mention the price, either—$1.

Actually, this statuette is a pretty sad article from an authentic characterization standpoint. Old Bill is swinging a lariat which certainly doesn't tie in very closely with his stock-in-trade. The hoss appears to be of a breed which one might see carved on the frieze of the Parthenon. The saddle is a joke. There are no stirrups and the leaves on the base of the casting look like flora that might be found somewhere deep in the Amazon. It's a first-class monstrosity insofar as artistic virtue is concerned, but the faults detract absolutely nothing from the historical significance of the object. In a way they tend to add a measure of primitive charm to it.

During midsummer of 1964, while browsing through a gift shop in Fort Worth, Texas, I came upon a circa 1964 reproduction of this same statuette! When gift specialty makers get to putting out replicas of this sort, it's a dog-gone sure sign that the original castings have an established collector appeal and considerable value to boot.

There are a half-dozen other figurines of the great showman, all somewhat similar in nature, which were peddled at the shows. One of them has always had a special appeal to me because of its true-to-life qualities. It depicts Buffalo Bill as a buckskin-clad hunter seated beside a stump, rifle in hand, scanning the prairie. The craftsman who executed this model achieved much more in the way of realism than is exemplified in the equestrian subject. The hunter statuette radiates a lot of western spirit and flavor that enhances its stature in the eyes of collectors.

When the Buffalo Bill-Pawnee Bill show folded up, the

66. This ten-inch-high, pot metal casting of Buffalo Bill was bought at a Wild West Show seventy-odd years ago. It cost $1.

remaining stock of these statuettes was sold to a clock wholesaler. Somehow or other, this feller had got himself stuck with a bunch of drab timepieces and he boxed his way out of a corner by mounting the statuettes atop his mantle clocks as ornamentation. In that manner, a considerable number of these statuettes found their way into homes that were far removed from the illustrious old showman's arena.

67. Buffalo Bill is portrayed with wonderful realism in this fine statuette. Here the illustrious old westerner is shown in his true role—hunter and scout.

A collector can shell out $45 for the equestrian statuette without the slightest qualm. In recognition of its finer craftsmanship, the hunter subject rates an extra $15 even though it appears to be no more scarce. The other subjects are mostly upright figurines of Buffalo Bill— rather like dolls. I saw one not long ago in an Americana

68. *"The Collector"—illustration by the author.*

dealer's catalog priced at $22.50. That's a fair evaluation for an item that warrants placement quite far up the scarcity ladder.

FOOD SAFE

AN ARTICLE APPEARED in a national publication a couple of years ago in which the author, an antique furniture authority, stated that a specific type of food safe (pie safe, some folks call it) should definitely be classified as a western type of kitchen furnishing. This assertion was surprising to me because I had never afforded those little kitchen cabinets anything more than casual interest. I felt they were no different from other pantry cabinets or cupboards which one might easily encounter anywhere from Maine to Montana—a General Americana sort of furnishing.

However, the gent who wrote that bit was absolutely right. He pointed out two significant differences between a safe made for the western market and those which were in general use elsewhere. Although very similar in design and overall construction, here's a rundown on the structural differences between the two types.

69. *Most western food safes (often called pie safes) have perforated tin ventilator panels on the sides and sometimes on the doors. This one, of golden oak, has thin wooden side ventilato₁s with typical Victorian designs depressed into the upper door panels.*

The frontier model has perforated side panels and, in some instances, perforated cabinet doors. These perforations were intended to facilitate the circulation of air throughout the cabinet interior. In arid regions, particularly in the Midwestern Plains and in the Southwest, proper ventilation of staples and other stored foods was of great importance. Panels were of light gauge tin with little holes pierced in decorative patterns similar to those a housewife makes with a fork on the top of pie crusts. Now and then a food safe will show up with very thin wooden panels, the holes having been made with a tiny drill. These features are entirely lacking in the eastern or General Americana version.

The other distinguishing aspect of the western cabinet was the wood employed in its construction. Usually it was made of woods such as pine, oak, ash or chestnut whereas the eastern types, intended for more pretentious interiors, were of walnut, cherry or finely-figured maple. Utilization of the more common cabinet woods was not because they possessed any particular qualities which were desirable or necessary in western climates—it was merely because the cabinets were made to sell cheaply. The hard-pressed homesteader needed a food storage container of some kind but couldn't afford anything very fancy.

Food safes were stocked in general stores along with other items required by a frontier community, and were priced at $7 or $8. The less costly wood contributed materially to the preservation of the homesteader's money pouch.

The cabinet was made to far less exacting standards than most articles of interior furnishing and, as a result, it's difficult to find one that isn't rickety. They were subjected to a lot of buffeting and the butt joint construction seldom withstood such treatment. Had dovetailing and lock joinery been employed, they would probably still be as sound as a Wells Fargo chest, but they were put together without much regard for the better principles of cabinetmaking.

It will be the exception rather than the rule to find a pie safe that isn't wobbly. But, in a sense, this condition can serve as an advantage to a collector of modest means because the shakiness of the cabinet should be compensated by a lower price tag. The one I have was mighty wobbly and awfully sad looking when I first saw it at a garage sale. It did have, however, two fine attributes: it was the real thing, and it had a very poor surface appearance which warranted no more, the owner figured, than a $4 price tag. The investment was so small I could hardly go wrong, so four ones were peeled off and I lugged it home.

A few well positioned finishing nails snugged up the butt joints. A couple of healthy applications of solvent removed a layer or two of grime, soot and the blistered, blackish crusting of several coats of varnish. Plenty of elbow grease with light sandpaper, and a dressing or two of polish transformed the old wreck into a beaming example of its former self.

If for no other reason, every Frontier Americana collector ought to have an old pie safe to display or store his miscellaneous collectables. It isn't often that a collector can kill two birds with one stone—acquiring a true frontier relic that will also serve a functional purpose. The shelves of mine are stacked with reference materials and the drawers house a collection of cartridges, bullet molds, military accouterments, old hand-forged nails, and, when I probe its depths, things I'd plumb forgotten I'd stashed away.

To top off these advantages pie safes are not too difficult to locate. In secondhand furniture stores and at auction barns, there are usually a couple of rickety specimens propped up in a corner somewhere. Unrestored, they're not overpriced at $25 to $35. If the used furniture feller has gone to the bother of reinforcing, refinishing or generally rehabilitating the cabinet, I suspect he'd have to ask close to $80 or $90 for it. However, an outlay of that amount will be money well spent. What other storage piece could you get at so modest a figure?

ARBUCKLES' COFFEE

IN MY INITIAL evaluation and selection of relics to be included in this book, I scratched off the Arbuckle brothers. It was not because those gents didn't rate a prominent place in the lore of the Old West; it was because I didn't have a single item to present in illustration of an Arbuckle relic—something that would be suitable for framing or display. Millions of pounds of Arbuckles' coffee had been sold to a couple of generations of Westerners; yet, after many years of collecting, I still hadn't found an Arbuckle coffee package, shipping case, advertising calendar, general store display sign, or anything else incident to the product which could appropriately be called a collector's item.

But, dadburnit, Arbuckles' coffee was just as much a part of western life as Winchesters and "bob-wire"! So out of sheer respect for the ole Arbuckle brothers, I've put them back in the book. I'll just leave it up to other collectors to find Arbuckle relics to be displayed in tribute to those two grand old fellers and their wonderful product.

It's a big challenge, too, because we're dealing primarily with a little paper bag, a one-pound package that had a premium coupon printed on its side. The snipping of those coupons for redemption to secure the famous Arbuckle premiums resulted in millions of cut up, and therefore, unsalvageable bags. Yet, I sorter figger a few of those old Arbuckle relics must be lurking around somewhere and if I plunk this "missing link" right squarely into the laps of other collectors, maybe someone can succeed where I've failed.

Prior to the 1870s, housewives bought their coffee in the only form generally available—the green state—far from ready for the coffee pot. It was necessary for folks to do their own roasting in the kitchen stove and unless this was handled just right, it resulted in scorching, waste, short tempers and a mess of other unsatisfactory aftermath.

John and Charles Arbuckle, wholesale grocery merchants of Pittsburgh, Pennsylvania, recognized the need to work out improvements in this hit-or-miss situation. John, somewhat more inclined toward experimentation than his brother, tackled the problem and proceeded to employ methods of roasting coffee in a scientifically controlled manner. Then he patented, in 1868, a process for coating the roasted beans with a sugar glaze which sealed the pores and thereby preserved the flavor and aroma of the coffee.

In 1873, Arbuckles' "Ariosa" coffee was introduced in little one-pound packages, "like peanuts." It's not known for sure what Ariosa stands for but one story explains it like this: "A" stands-for Arbuckle, the "rio" for Rio and the "sa" for South America or Santos—Rio and Santos coffees being varieties that were combined in the original blend.

It's almost impossible to even "guesstimate" the value of a neat little Ariosa bag, an Arbuckle premium list, a tin store sign or calendar, or any one of a dozen other things comprising the merchandising paraphernalia of the renowned Arbuckle concern. Probably not more than $8 or $10 for any one of them, I suppose. But the point is, the Arbuckle brothers were closely linked to the western scene and a display of Frontier Americana seems to be a mite incomplete without something to reflect the predominant position they occupied in kitchens, around campfires and at chuck wagons throughout the West for sixty years or more. Like sourdough biscuits and son-of-a-gun stew, Arbuckles' coffee was an institution and it's a cryin' shame that I haven't been able to find a ding-busted thing associated with it.

If, as a result of this little salute, some collector happens to find an old Ariosa bag that has been tucked away in the far corner of a long forgotten kitchen cabinet, I hope he'll afford it a snug little place of its own in a display cabinet. Offhand I can't think of another relic that has more right to be there.

ANGLE LAMP

"The Light That Never Fails" was the trade slogan adopted by the New York firm that produced Angle lamps. It was a clever slogan and their lamps were of exceptionally fine quality. A lot of other lampmakers were wheeling and dealing around the big cities back East, however, and Angle lamps didn't seem to move off tradesmens' shelves with any degree of regularity. Since the slogan wasn't clicking with those eastern folks, a new approach had to be devised if the Angle lamp people were going to stay in business. Somebody hit upon the idea that points westward offered a more promising outlet, so the firm directed its merchandising efforts in that direction. It was a smart move.

One could almost trace the routes of the itinerant peddlers along a fairly wide belt from St. Louis to Salt Lake City by noting the appearance of these unique lamps. The outcome of the venture resulted in the Angle lamp gaining such wide acceptance in many western communities that it may properly be designated as a "western" fixture.

During the late 1880s and early 1890s when gas illumination and the incandescent bulb began to take over in the more heavily populated areas, oil lamp outfits folded up right and left. But the Angle lamp people had gotten out in time and had a fair grip on the western trade. They held on tight. The bossman at the Angle Lamp Company was acutely aware of what interested the Westerner and he never missed an opportunity to spot his advertising where western folks would see it.

Even as late as 1901, the Company was advertising in *Collier's Weekly* which had a large circulation beyond the Mississippi. This was during the period when *Collier's* was featuring the writing of prominent western authors and carrying on its covers and as full-color double-page spreads inside the superb western illustration of Frederic Remington.

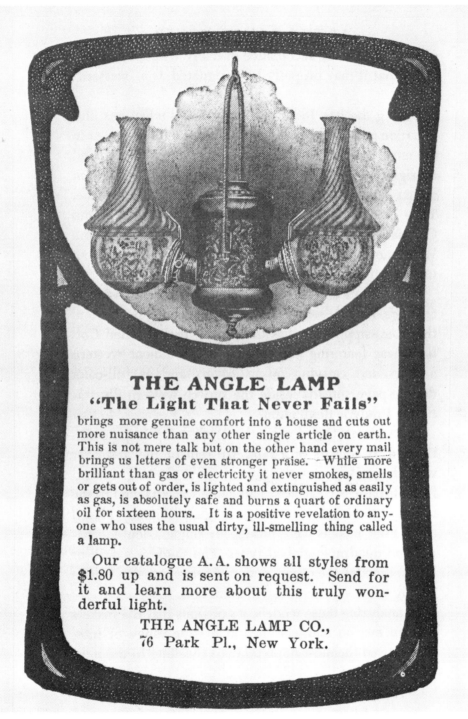

70. *A double-globed Angle lamp is shown in this advertisement which appeared in* Collier's Weekly *for January 26, 1901.*

In its elementary design, the Angle lamp is quite distinctive. It consists of a tank-like font or fuel reservoir with the wick placed as a sort of spout slanting upward from its base. A clear glass ball globe was attached to the

71. This wall-type Angle lamp, complete with milk glass chimney, was priced at $1.80 when originally offered during the late 1890s. The font or fuel tank is lacquered tin.

rim of the wick unit with a milk glass chimney placed atop. Four models were produced: single-, double-, triple and quadruple-globed types. The single is a wall or bracket model, the others designed for suspension from a ceiling to provide overhead illumination.

In analyzing these models, it's obvious that the makers had an eye on marketability in a wide range of interiors—from the most unpretentious dwelling to the most exclusive parlors and hotel lobbies. The larger multiple-globed models, with ornately embossed brass or silver plated fonts, are beautiful things. By monetary standards then, they were quite expensive—from $15 to $20. The single-globe model, undecorated, with heavy tin font sold for $1.80.

In scanning through my notebooks, I find some revealing jottings concerning the present-day prevalence of these fine lamps. In parts of the Midwest (the western portion of Missouri, Kansas and Nebraska), they appear to be quite numerous. More than twenty examples were observed in shops throughout that region. From there they fan out in diminishing numbers: three in Texas, two in northeastern New Mexico, two in Colorado, three in Arkansas, and one in Louisiana. This pattern of distribution seems to indicate an exclusive territory in which the company concentrated its marketing operations. With all the relocation and transient activity that has occurred in recent years, Angle lamps may appear in shops from Florida to Oregon, but the Midwest is more or less "home" to them.

A collector friend and I were discussing these lamps one evening. He remarked that he had once seen a single-globe Angle lamp in a caboose mounted on a wall directly over the little table-like affair the conductor used as a desk. How it got there is no great mystery because we know some western railroad administrators purchased Angle lamps for use in depots and yard offices. But the thing that's puzzling is how the milk glass chimney could have survived the shuntings and jarrings of the caboose in the workaday business of railroading.

The conductor must have taken a fancy to that particular type of lamp and rigged up some method of fastening the chimney securely to the ball globe to keep it from tottering off. The lamp was never designed for utilization in moving vehicles, much less the jolt and jar of railroad rolling stock. Nevertheless, there it was—in a caboose—and it demonstrates that many objects were adapted to uses and places far removed from the purpose and location for which they were primarily intended. It wouldn't surprise me in the least if someone recovered an old Angle lamp from the cabin of a derelict riverboat somewhere up in the Yukon. It doesn't belong there, but it just might be there, anyway.

Prices are quite consistent with those of most other quality kerosene lamps that were produced during the latter part of the last century. The wall-type or bracket Angle lamp can usually be secured for $30 to $40. Doubles bring $85 and the last triple I saw was priced at $150. The "Big Four," a more scarce model than the others,

should be well worth $225. As with other antiques in which several components are involved, these prices apply to lamps complete with their original clear glass ball globes and milk glass chimneys.

WINCHESTER '66 "YELLOW BOY"

IT WAS SIDELINE dabbling that got Oliver Winchester into the firearms business in a big way. He had a thriving shirt manufacturing business going at New Haven, Connecticut, back in the 1850s and profits were piling up something fierce. Gunmakers were plentiful up around those parts and they all seemed to be making a go of it,

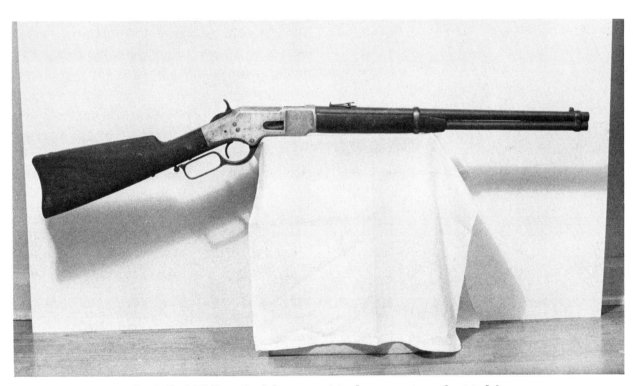

72. Called "Yellow Boy" because of its brass receiver, the Model 1866 Winchester was one of the most popular guns of the Old West. It was a .44 caliber gun made for both rimfire and centerfire and preceded the famous Model 1873 Winchester.

so Winchester diverted some of his shirt-making profits into an outfit known as the New Haven Arms Company. He also bought eighty of the six hundred shares of common stock in the Volcanic Repeating Arms Company (at $25 per share!). Anyway, Oliver Winchester soon found himself up to his ears in the gun business and even though he knew next to nothing about firearms, he had a man named B. Tyler Henry on his payroll who did.

Henry had fiddled around with the rimfire metallic cartridge idea and in 1860 came up with one that was a humdinger. Having perfected it, he proceeded to make a rifle to shoot it. The introduction of the Henry rifle, with its .44 caliber cartridge, opened up an entirely new field in the firearms industry with Mr. Winchester sitting right in the middle of it. During the Civil War the company prospered and by the time the conflict was over, Winchester had a clear fix on the gun market and reorganized his setup under the name of the Winchester Repeating Arms Company.

The new company started off in 1866 with the production of a new weapon, the first rifle to actually bear the Winchester name. It was an improved adaptation of the Henry rifle, chambered for his .44 caliber rimfire cartridge and employing a tubular magazine fitted to produce repeating fire by means of a lever action. This was the famous Winchester Model 1866, aptly dubbed "Yellow Boy" because of its shiny brass frame. It soon became a great favorite with Westerners because of its simple, fast-loading principle and the fact that it could be easily carried on horseback. The sideloading gate was uncomplicated and the trim weapon delivered a hefty fire power that was reasonably appropriate to frontier business-in-hand. Before the model was eventually discontinued, 170,000 had been sold.

Everybody was happy: Oliver Winchester made a wagonload of dough; Henry, the plant superintendent, was happily ramrodding his gunsmiths; and the Westerner had a rifle he was proud to own.

Whenever I hear someone use the expression "Great Guns!" I try to hazard a guess as to where it originated. I'd like to think it emanated somewhere on the frontier where a new shipment of "Yellow Boys" was being unloaded at a trading post. They were "Great Guns" all right and, if the expression didn't originate there, it should have.

When you look at the big success story in retrospect, it's almost impossible to see how it could have missed. The concoction had all three ingredients necessary to make it a winner: an improved firearm, a means of producing it in quantity at a decent price, and a rifleman who liked it.

Not long ago I spotted a near perfect example of the Winchester '66 listed in the catalog of a prominent Americana dealer. After viewing the illustration and reading the commentary regarding its condition, serial number data and so forth, my eye bounced along a row of dots to the price column. The $325 bit printed there made me blink a time or two and I think I muttered something like "Great Guns!"

They're high—but they're mighty!

TABLE OF VALUES

The column on the right denotes the degree of scarcity of each relic. The numbers assign a scarcity factor as follows: 1–3 common, 4–6 scarce, 7–9 rare.

Relic	Fair	Good	Excellent	Scarcity Factor
Angle Lamp				
Single Globe (Wall)	$ 25	$35+	$ 50	5
Double Globe	$ 40	$ 65	$ 85–95	5
Triple Globe	$ 60+	$ 95+	$150+	6
Quadruple Globe	$ 90	$165+	$225–250+	7
Arbuckle's Coffee (Ariosa package, advertising calendar, packing case, store sign, premium list, etc.)	$ 4.50	$ 7.50	$ 10–12	5
Buffalo Bill				
Statuettes				
Horse and Rider	$ 20	$ 30+	$ 45+	5
Hunter and Scout	$ 30	$ 50	$ 60+	5
Other	$ 15	$ 20	$ 30+	5
Food Safe (Pie Safe)				
Restored	$ 30+	$ 50	$ 90–100	2
Unrestored	$ 20	$ 30+	$ 45+	3
Winchester '66 "Yellow Boy"	$100	$200	$350	7

AT THE GOLDEN NUGGET

73. *Unlike the showy, sometimes pretentious hard spirits emporiums of Long Branch renown, most frontier bars were of rude construction and seldom deserving to be termed "saloon." Frederic Remington's illustration for a story appearing in* Harper's New Monthly Magazine *shows a range rider demanding that other indispensable western product administered over the bar— justice.*

WHISKEY CANTEEN

Just a few short years ago, the relicker who spent a weekend probing around abandoned farms, remote settlements or early campsites could expect to bring home any number of bottles, jugs, jars, demijohns—all kinds of glass and earthenware containers. The back country abounded in them. When I first began collecting frontier relics, I toted home every old booze bottle and jug I could lay my hands on but soon had to call a halt because of space limitations. There must have been a Conestoga wagonload of them that I was forced to leave behind.

The picture now is entirely changed. Bottle bugs by the thousands have taken to the road—all over the country. Handbooks, guidebooks and reference pamphlets devoted to bottles and jugs have stimulated a tremendous activity in this area of collector interest. In browsing over these publications, I find that some of the flasks, patent medicine and bitters bottles I had to pass up are scarce as geese teeth now. I have no regrets, though. I still got in on the game when the pickin's were mighty good.

I have one item, in particular, a beautiful canteen-shaped whiskey jug, that is a magnificent example of the potter's craft. It was found a few years ago in an abandoned prairie cellar (a twister shelter) in central Kansas. There was an additional thrill connected with the finding of this jug—I witnessed the "birth" of a new collector. For quite some time I had prided myself with having developed a keen eye toward spotting things of this nature, but that autumn morning I had explored the cellar from one end to the other and found absolutely nothing. I was crawling out toward the sunshine when my son, who was following behind me, suddenly said, "Hey, Pops! Lookie here!" There, big as life in his hands, was the old canteen-shaped whiskey jug. He was plumb tickled with the discovery and it made me beam all over, too. For him, more than the relic.

The jug is of earthenware, about sixteen inches high, with its surface highly glazed a rich, deep brown. The detailing of the looped handle and base is so well crafted that it's obvious the vessel was made to accommodate a quality whiskey—one full gallon of it. A handsome molded inscription adds tremendously to the historic appeal of the relic since it identifies the name of the product and city of origin—"Quinn's Rye Whiskey, Kansas City, Missouri."

Finding something that bears the maker's name and place of business is always of interest because it opens the door for further exploration into the background and significance of the object. Frequently, particularly if paper were used, an intriguing part of the story can never be known because of the missing label.

In running down data connected with my jug, I

Vinegar jugs and "little brown jugs" are still to be found in many rural communities but canteen-shaped whiskey jugs are scarce. As with all items of crockery, glass and other fragile materials, it's doubly hard to find one that's sound throughout. Minor chips, therefore, are to be afforded a degree of tolerance. Providing the small looped handle and base are intact, $35 is not too much to shell out for one.

GAME TABLE LAMP

THERE WAS A heap of goin's on after sundown in frontier communities three or four generations ago, and most of those nocturnal affairs were conducted under the yaller glow of lanterns and lamps. Lamps and more lamps of every conceivable style and type floodlighted the great West. Coal oil was just about as much a staple at trading

74. *Found in an abandoned prairie cellar in central Kansas, this beautifully crafted, canteen-shaped whiskey jug has added historic appeal in its handsome molded inscription.*

learned that a miniature of it, about five or six inches tall (a sort of sample or gift), was always placed in the straw-packed case containing eight of the regular gallon canteens. Why eight, I never could find out. Six or twelve per case would, for invoice or manifest purposes, be pretty decent figures to bat around in the bookkeeping, but eight it was—two-thirds of a dozen. As for the miniatures, the only one I've seen was in a display case at Pioneer Village, Minden, Nebraska, in 1962.

Old advertising literature confirms that western railroad lines and even jerkline freighters hauled a good many cases of these fine canteen jugs out of terminal points during the homestead era.

75. *A game table lamp is a good example of a relic that frequently has to be recovered piece by piece. This font represents one-third of the complete unit; still to be located are the frame and shade.*

posts and general stores as was flour, beans or cartridges.

Most of these lamps, of course, were of a type in general use everywhere at that time—Argand, Rayo and pedestal-type table lamps of similar design were peddled by the carloads from coast to coast. Even the fancier Victorian parlor lamps, generally referred to as "Gone With The Wind" lamps, graced the interiors of many western residences. The collector who can't seem to secure a nice old kerosene lamp hasn't been trying too hard. Unless, of course, he wants a lamp that looks western.

There is one—a type of lamp that fits in with western surroundings in such a manner as to appear almost out of place in any other setting. I call it a "game table" lamp.

It's a small, rabbit-eared, green-shaded font that is frequently shown suspended over a saloon game table or from a cabin rafter. This little gem looks and acts so much the part of a frontier "character," that western illustrators rarely paint a saloon interior without including one. If it's a western lamp you've got to have, this is about as close as you'll come.

There aren't very many of them around anymore and the reasons are not difficult to explain. First, they were cheaply made, usually of tin or low grade brass. When the day of kerosene had run its course, these lamps were the first to be junked, primarily because they had no decorative qualities to warrant retention for display. They had never been accepted in polite society, so their tale of woe is simply that they didn't have what it takes to survive in the world of old lamps where color, charm and beauty are considered the criteria of worth.

To find a complete one is a rough assignment. My lamp has been silently awaiting a reunion with its long lost kin (frame and shade) for three years. This is just another example of a relic that frequently has to be recovered bit by bit—the chimney, here, the shade there, and so on. It is equally true of the finer Victorian parlor lamps. The ball shade is often a mismatch, or the spider

has been lost or stolen. At any rate, if any single component can be secured, it'll start the ball rolling and perhaps a complete, authentic old game table lamp will be the outcome of vigilant pursuit.

Considering $25 to $30 as a fair price for the entire relic, a piece by piece breakdown would look something like this: font $8, frame $7, shade $6, chimney $3, burner $2.

WESTERN ART

THERE HAVE BEEN many fourth rate performances purporting to represent the role played by the frontier saloon in the western community. One basic formula prescribes huge doses of violent action, permitting only two things to happen around such an establishment: a general busting up of the premises by uncouth, hard-drinking brawlers and fantastically accurate lead-slinging with its resultant litter of shot-up tinhorns and desperadoes.

Actually, no saloonkeeper could have stayed in business a week under such conditions. The fact that most western saloons were both first and last on the scene is conclusive testimony that the proprietors exercised efficient control over the operation of their places and the conduct of their patrons.

The truth of the matter is, the frontier saloon came far closer to being a social center or fraternal headquarters than the hangout for thieves and killers. And, don't snicker at this, the western saloon later became a cultural center. It was a place where sound, progressive decisions were made concerning community welfare, and often a gallery for displaying creative arts that were produced by some of the more inspired citizenry.

The first saloon to be set up at a frontier settlement usually consisted of nothing more than a tent or tarpaulin shelter. The interior was furnished with crates or shipping cases providing a sort of bar with benches or kegs for seats. Off in a corner, the whiskey barrel was set in a sawbuck-type rack with tin cups hung from a slat nearby. That was it! No decor or culture about the place—just an old freighter sitting in a corner with his pipe and cup, chatting in a low drawl with the barkeeper.

A dozen trips later, the freighter might pull up, get down from his wagon seat and enter the Golden Nugget to greet and chat with his barkeep friend. This time he might stand at a polished bar and look across at his tired, weathered features reflected in an ornately framed mirror. He might spot, too, a vivid pattern of color reflected in the corner of the mirror—something on the wall behind him—a colorful painting of men and horses.

"That's a right nice piece of work," the barkeep might volunteer, "done by a feller who rides for the Circle A." The freighter, a gent who has seen a lot of men and horses, would agree that it was "plumb good."

Neither the barkeep nor the freighter were concerned about the artist's prospects of achieving international fame as a painter of the American West, but some whose first works were displayed in frontier saloons did attain world recognition. Just as the writings of some of our finest western authors were first published by territorial presses, many of the initial works of great western artists were first displayed and bargained for at those unlikely "galleries" named The Mint, The Silver Dollar and the Golden Nugget.

Two names have become almost synonymous with fine western art: Frederic Remington and Charles M. Russell. These men have long been recognized as unparalleled giants of the profession—"Old Masters" of the craft. Both deserve such distinction because of their finer accomplishments; on occasion, however, both turned out uninspired stuff—the type thing subtle art critics refer to as "minor works" or, as one art historian appropriately captioned one of Remington's paintings, "Although this is not the master at his best . . ." But by and large, the two

big "Rs" produced work that embraced the highest standards of artistic excellence.

Remington and Russell didn't do everything in their field, however—not by a long shot. They didn't, nor did they hope to, nail a lid on the crate and ship it off as a filled order. Relatively early on the scene, their prolific output has contributed mightily toward capturing and preserving the feel of the Old West, but there were several others whose works comprise equally outstanding contributions.

One in particular, Newell Converse Wyeth, has done some superb paintings—works that rank in every respect with the best of Remington and Russell. And, to comment briefly on an important factor concerning collector value, N. C. Wyeth's masterpieces can be bought today for far less than the price of "minor works" by one of the big "Rs."

Newell Converse Wyeth was born at Needham, Massachusetts, a small community outside Boston, on October 22, 1882. During his teens he attended an art academy in Boston and a fair measure of significance must be afforded to the work he did there. It showed real promise and shortly thereafter he was admitted to a select circle of students assembled at the studio of Howard Pyle in Wilmington, Delaware. Pyle, one of the most eminent of American illustrators, exerted a strong influence upon young Wyeth and it was not long before he had a firm grip on the essentials of the craft.

As with all students, there came the day when the teacher extended a farewell handshake and expressed all good wishes as his pupil sallied forth into the big, wide world to make his mark.

The color and drama of the Old West had a particular appeal to young Wyeth and it is not too surprising that his initial venture was westward. He went into the region of Little Rattlesnake Creek, Cottonwood Camp and Jim's Cañon, Colorado, in the early summer of 1904.

The twenty-two-year-old illustrator spent some four or

five months in that cattle country and produced a remarkable series of paintings, several of which are reproduced in this book. To accompany these illustrations, he wrote a brief article entitled "A Day With The Round-Up," which appeared in *Scribner's Magazine* for March, 1906.

76. N. C. Wyeth, distinguished American illustrator, Colorado, 1904.

N. C. Wyeth was much more than a pictorial recorder; he was a painter's painter, one of those gifted individuals whose paintings radiated an atmosphere, the very substance and texture of things, the actual shouts and smells. His gunsmoke isn't simply blue-gray paint on canvas—it has the effect of actual, pungent wisps of burnt powder smoke. His dust isn't just earthy pigment; it's almost as if real alkaline dust has adhered to the canvas.

A superb colorist, Wyeth's tones are always rich in dusty tans, muted greens and warm shades of sandy ochre—real "western" colors. There's a swarthiness about his cattlemen that reflects long exposure to the elements. We know the wrangler was partial to vivid neckerchiefs and jackets. Wyeth's treatment of these fabrics does not depict the newness of recent purchase, but rather the well-faded, soiled tonal values of long, hard use. The excellence of his brushmanship extends even to the "smell" of leather and animals—and his parched, gnarled mesquite tree exudes an aroma completely its own.

This texturing is what makes an illustrator a great painter. Winslow Homer had it. So did Remington. These qualities in Wyeth's painting attained the highest plateau of achievement and justify his position as a painter's painter.

Another thing about Wyeth, he was consistently good. I've never seen a painting or an illustration by N. C. Wyeth that fell below an impressive degree of accomplishment and I doubt if there is one.

Sometime ago, I spent the better part of a week in Taos, New Mexico, studying the works of our western illustrators in several private galleries. A painting by N. C. Wyeth, originally reproduced in *Scribner's Magazine* as an illustration for a story about outlaws and sheriffs, was on display with a $4,000 tag. At another gallery I saw a Wyeth illustration of a gunfight at a frontier bar—the price $3,500. When an art dealer places a four-figure tab on a painting, I'd say that particular illustrator enjoys a prominent reputation in serious art circles.

Most of us can't afford the luxury of owning an original painting by N. C. Wyeth. However, there's a next-best approach to the subject. To acquire the original printings of these fine works (first editions, so to speak) is still within the scope of our pocketbooks. This first printing facet of western art collecting means acquiring the book

77. *Wyeth had a keenness for showing the cowboy at a task not usually portrayed. In this painting, he depicts the roper during those moments before he was mounted for a day of riding and roping.*

or periodical in which the work of a distinguished illustrator was first reproduced. As an example, if a collector can secure a copy of *Collier's* for April 20, 1901, he will have, in the center spread of the magazine, a sixteen- by twenty-two-inch print of a Frederic Remington painting entitled "A Monte Game At The Southern Ute Agency." This reproduction is the publication debut of that particular work. That painting may have been reproduced in other books and magazines a hundred times since 1901, but the initial presentation is a collector's item.

78. *"The Silent Fisherman," painted in 1906, demonstrates Wyeth's remarkable ability to convey mood. In this work, the serenity and dramatic quietness is in stark contrast to the tremendous force and vigor of his wild cattle, mustangs and hell-for-leather riders.*

Historical societies and gallery librarians have been picking up early copies of *Collier's, Scribner's, Harper's, McClure's* and similar periodicals in which the original reproductions of works by those illustrators who have contributed measurably to the art of the Old West appeared.

In used book shops there are still early editions of western novels which contain many of Wyeth's finest western illustrations. I can predict, with a reasonable degree of certainty, that these first printings of Wyeth's illustrations will eventually be as sought after by established collectors as the original printings of Remington and Russell illustrations are.

A comprehensive listing of books and magazines containing the initial publication of N. C. Wyeth's western art would be far too extensive to include here, but a few titles can be given to steer collectors in the right direction. *Vandemark's Folly* by Herbert Quick and the 1907 edition of *Bar-20* by Clarence E. Mulford contain some remarkably fine black and white illustrations. *Langford of the Three Bars* by Kate and Virgil D. Boyles and *Arizona Nights* by Stewart Edward White (both carry 1907 dates) have superb color plates. *Whispering Smith* by Frank H. Spearman is another title to watch for. *Buffalo Bill's Life Story,* published in 1920 by the Cosmopolitan Book Corporation and *Jinglebob* by Philip Ashton Rollins (1930), although more recent, are still well worth buying and preserving. Old copies of *Scribner's Magazine,* especially the 1906 to 1915 editions, are a treasure house of great Wyeth illustrations.

I'm sure many oldtimers will remember a general store poster put out in 1907 by the Cream of Wheat people. It showed a western postman astride a sleepy pony at a prairie crossroads placing a letter in a mailbox. The wooden box, nailed atop a post, has "Cream of Wheat" stenciled on its side. A good copy of this N. C. Wyeth **painting currently brings $25 to $30 at print galleries.**

I have for good purpose, I believe, made the works of N. C. Wyeth the principal ingredient in this little discourse on western art. A dozen books have been done on Remington and Russell and their story has been well told but, so far as I know, the tremendous accomplishments of N. C. Wyeth have not yet been publicized and that's where the collector gets in on the ground floor. If he can afford them, he can secure original works at about the same prices Russell's and Remington's work commanded twenty-five or thirty years ago.

The stampede for "a Wyeth" isn't yet underway, but it will be, shore as shootin', because of one factor: his greatness is evident in every western subject he painted. Look at a Remington for $25,000, then look at a Wyeth for $5,000 or $7,500. The only difference is in the price tag, not in the quality.

A couple of months ago I secured a booklet which listed important museums and collections in the State of Texas and what they offered in the way of interest to tourists. For the first time, to my knowledge, a gallery boasting of its attractions concludes with "and paintings by such distinguished western painters as Remington, Russell and *Wyeth.*" It seems that my opinion of Wyeth's ability is finally being shared.

This great illustrator died in 1945. American art—western art in particular—has been left a tremendous legacy in the hundreds of masterful works that came from his brush. And, he has left us still more.

Just as N. C. Wyeth had carried forward the tradition of purposeful and accomplished illustration as taught to him by Howard Pyle, so did he, in turn, teach and strongly influence two of the most eminent painters in America today—Andrew Wyeth and Peter Hurd. A few years ago, Andrew Wyeth achieved a distinction unique in the history of American art—the sale of one of his paintings for $58,000, the highest price ever recorded for a work by a living American painter. Peter Hurd, N. C. Wyeth's son-in-law and an internationally famous painter, muralist, illustrator and lithographer, needs no

79. Painted in 1906, N. C. Wyeth's postman is a splendid example of western art as applied to the advertising poster.

introduction whatsoever. He has reached the summit of prominence in the field of western painting and both Fred Remington and Charlie Russell would, I'm sure, be the first to acknowledge that Hurd's stature in western art is not in the least exaggerated.

I cannot say with certainty that N. C. Wyeth's paintings were ever displayed in frontier saloons as were those of Remington and Russell. Probably not. But there had to be a setting or locale for the works of budding western painters and the walls of the Golden Nugget made a far more logical display space than did the palatial residence of a bonanza king.

There were many others who did magnificent western painting—men whose works can hold their own with the very best that has been produced.

Two, in particular, are Harvey Dunn and Frank E. Schoonover (like Wyeth, students of Howard Pyle). Allen True, Maynard Dixon, W. H. Dunton, Frank Tenney Johnson and Gayle Hoskins have all done superb work in the field. Will Crawford, a brilliant pen and ink artist and, incidentally, a close friend of Charlie Russell, did some of the finest black and white westerns that have ever appeared in American illustration. He is regarded by critics as the Rembrandt of western illustration by virtue of his fine, etching-like style. And there are others: Frank Hoffman, Charles Hargens, Nick Eggenhofer—and a dozen more.

The pages of old periodicals and pulp-paper thrillers of thirty or forty years ago are loaded with reproductions of the finest works of these distinguished illustrators and the beautiful part of it all is that the door is still wide open to securing first printings from those sources. Old issues of *Harper's, Scribner's, Ace High, Adventure, Street and Smith's Western, Top Notch Western*—I could go on through fifty titles or more, but the collector has to take over from here and pan the rich outcropping for himself.

Practically every western novel or pulp thriller of yes-

80. *Almost every western illustrator has, at one time or another, portrayed the bronc rider. Wyeth painted "Bucking" at Jim's Canōn, Colorado, in 1904.*

terday will yield something in the way of fine western illustration, and a portfolio of clips from those old magazines will, in time, be of tremendous historical and artistic value. If ever a collector had an opportunity to form his own private gallery of "the best of the West," this is it!

A few words about value. There's no way under the sun to arrive at a standard criterion for ascribing a set price to an original painting by N. C. Wyeth, Fred Remington, Winslow Homer—or anyone else, for that matter. This is an area of responsibility I'll gladly relinquish to the men who should know and *do* know—established art dealers, gallery directors and museum curators.

As for first printings, value is not nearly so difficult to determine although there are some variables. An old *Century*, for example, that contains fine illustrations by

TABLE OF VALUES

The column on the right denotes the degree of scarcity of each relic. The numbers assign a scarcity factor as follows: 1–3 common, 4–6 scarce, 7–9 rare.

Relic	Fair	Good	Excellent	Scarcity Factor
Game Table Lamp				
Burner			$ 1.50	2
Chimney		$ 2	$ 3	3
Font	$ 3.50	$ 5	$ 6.50	5
Frame	$ 3	$ 4.50	$ 6	5
Shade	$ 4.50	$ 6	$ 8.50	4
Complete	$14	$20+	$32.50	6
Western Art*				
First Printings				
Pulp-paper				
Periodicals				
1915–1930	$ 2	$ 3.50–4	$6–7.50	
Slick-paper				
Periodicals				
1890–1920	$ 2.50	$ 3.50–4	$ 6–8	
Hardback Novels	$ 2.50	$ 3.50–4	$ 7.50	5
Original Works				
Whiskey Canteen	$15	$22.50	$45	7

* Assigning a scarcity factor and specific value to an old periodical is exceedingly difficult. Each one must be judged on its own merit. Whereas one pulp-paper western may contain a dozen or more outstanding western illustrations, another issue of the same publication may contain none. Well-known authors also figure prominently in determining value. The prices shown here are for magazines that contain some "meat."

Remington is worth $6 or $8—certainly not much more. *Century* was a quality magazine and a good many were preserved, so it's just a matter of finding them in bookshops and secondhand stores. They're around but they won't be forever, and the same goes for pulp thrillers and hardback western novels of 1900 to 1920.

The collector may find a nice copy of a Zane Grey novel with fine western illustrations in a bookshop. The dealer may ask $4 for it, but the collector could just as easily locate the same work at a rummage sale for a dime. I realize this value span has its inconsistencies but gold is where you find it—in a creek bed or in a jeweler's shop.

AND THERE'S MORE...

AND STILL MORE. The lore of the Old West embraces so many distinctive and colorful things that were significant to its history and development there's virtually no point where a feller can draw the line and say, "That's the crop!" There's always another wonderful old fragment of frontier life and times that will pop up and clamor for recognition—an object that will be just as deserving of inclusion as all the others.

I could have included a chapter entitled "At The Sod House" in which items intimately associated with sodbusters' ways and means were presented and evaluated. Many of the accessories utilized by soddies and homesteaders are of a definite prairie character, to be found only in midwestern regions. The sodbuster's plow, for example, more than any other single implement, transformed millions of acres of buffalo grazing grounds into a sea of grain. I wonder how many folks know of or have ever seen a wire stretcher? Yet, it was prevalent throughout the Great Plains wherever barbed wire was being strung and, so far as I've been able to learn, was never marketed anywhere else.

In my rovings through abandoned prairie cellars, I've collected a fascinating group of containers that practically relate the complete story of frontier canning—the "putting up" of foods to sustain those hardy pioneers through the long, hard winters. One of those unique pieces of pottery is a preserves jar—a one pint container—completely of earthenware even to the wavy threads at its collar. Those threads were fashioned to accommodate a zinc screw cap of the same type used on the original Mason jar—the 1858 patent type with bubbly, irregularly molded glass of a beautiful deep aqua. There are jars, also of earthenware, with stout wire clamp devices for fastening lids in an airtight seal. I once found a very old pottery funnel, a jar funnel, which was used to facilitate the pouring operation at canning time. Every one of those jars contributed its bit toward the winning of the West and, lowly though one may appear, it still has a whopping lot to say about life on the frontier.

Many years ago, when I first began browsing around

81. Barbed wire stretcher patented in 1883.

old frontier sites, mine was a one-track mind. I concentrated my relic hunting to areas around abandoned wagonsheds, bunkhouses, barns, prairie cellars and the like. I was actually blind to certain significant relics that were silhouetted way off on the prairie horizon—completely away, for the most part, from habitable structures. Later I discovered them, limestone fenceposts, unique objects of prairie Americana. They played an his-

earliest uses to which it was put was for dugouts of buffalo hunters. Later, because of its availability and abundance, homesteaders employed post rock for such structures as schools, churches, bridges, homes and storm shelters. The fencepost is probably the most unusual form to which limestone was adapted, and it is estimated that about forty thousand miles of post rock fence can be traced throughout central Kansas.

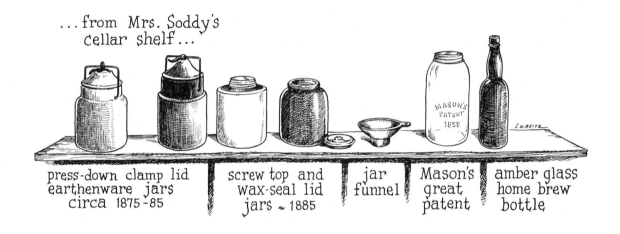

... from Mrs. Soddy's cellar shelf...

press-down clamp lid earthenware jars circa 1875-85   screw top and wax-seal lid jars ~ 1885   jar funnel   Mason's great patent   amber glass home brew bottle

toric role in the lore of the Kansas sodbuster. I say *Kansas* sodbuster because that is the only locale on our prairie frontier where these wonderful relics appear.

Since the 1870s, limestone fenceposts have supported barbed wire around thousands of acres in north-central Kansas. Many of them still stand guard today, reflecting the ingenuity of the pioneers who conceived and erected them on those almost treeless acres. No two posts are quite alike in size, shape or in the subtle hues that time and nature have weathered on their surfaces.

Limestone was uncovered from outcroppings, "sledged" out by hand, and dressed with stone hammers for use in all sorts of prairie construction. One of the

An average post is five and one-half to six feet in length, set in the ground eighteen to twenty-four inches, and weighs several hundred pounds. Corner posts often exceed a half ton. About a foot in width at the bottom (many are more narrow at the top) and some eight inches thick, their irregularity is the result of varying rock formation and the care and pride taken in quarrying.

Holes were drilled into the limestone strata at eight inch intervals and wedges were placed in the holes. Light pounding caused the rock to split in the desired width. In winter, water was sometimes poured in the holes and the expansion of the freezing water would split the stone.

83. A central Kansas limestone fencepost. These two-toned light tan, rusty-brown posts with weathered, dark, irregular patches dress the prairie landscape with a distinctiveness not found elsewhere.

The quarrying of limestone for fenceposts was discontinued many years ago when wood and steel posts were made available at a much lower cost.

I realize a feller can't go around digging up five-hundred-pound monoliths to lug home for lawn display or patio decoration—even those with a "pioneer personality." The essential purpose in mentioning them at all is to show the enormous scope and variety of men's efforts to adjust to a new environment, and a harsh one, at that.

*84. Post rock limestone was used in the construction of this early
prairie dugout in central Kansas. The flooding of Wilson Reservoir
will soon obliterate it from the frontier scene.*

A section devoted to the sheriff's office would have included such interesting items as lawman's badges, shackles and leg irons, "Wanted" posters, execution invitations and a dozen more things one could expect to find around such a place.

Some of the old territorial laws required that a few citizens witness and verify public execution of criminals. Western prison officials quite often prepared some downright elaborately engraved cards announcing the place, date and hour prescribed. Those little admission tickets are now scarce as clean socks in a bunkhouse.

A grand old cowboy pal of mine, Hackberry "Slim"

Johnson, recently gave me a dome-knocker that had been used by a deputy marshal in South Texas many years ago. I wouldn't say it's a charming thing to look at, but it certainly did its part to convince wayward waddies that the deputy meant exactly what he said. Both the execution "invite" and the dome-knocker qualify admirably for acceptance as true Frontier Americana.

"At the Line Camp" would have afforded an opportunity to include many more articles necessary to the cowboy's gear—holsters, cuffs (wristlets, they're sometimes called), riatas, quirts, bandannas, vests, boots, chaps and a lot of other things made out of rawhide and leather. In a less perishable category, I've found some nice hand-wrought fireplace accessories around deserted line shacks—blacksmith-forged pokers and andirons mostly, and some early handmade bricks from their crumbling chimneys. All these things are old, truly western, and history-laden.

The story of the Old West is, to a great extent, the biography of thousands of mules and hosses. "At the Blacksmith's Shop" would certainly have been an appropriate setting to cover the several tools of the trade in that craftsman's establishment. Isn't the "smithy box" shown here a Jim Dandy? It was found in the hayloft of an old livery stable near Abilene. What could be a more subtle reminder of that rip-roaring town during its heyday a hundred years ago? The bull's-eye lantern was there, but the eight-hour day wasn't! Many a smithy worked long into the night under the beam of that old lantern to make ready a coach or rig which had to depart on schedule at daybreak. And many a soddy milked his cow at dawn in the glow of one just like it.

Speaking of lanterns, how about the switchman's and brakeman's squat little lanterns—the early ones with "UPRR" marked on the hat-like canopy over the globe? Union Pacific is as much a synonym for "West" as Wells Fargo.

Another item that spells "West," though perhaps in

85. *Since they were handmade, hardly any two stone post drills are alike. Used like a brace and bit, the weight of the heavy iron wheel kept pushing the bit down into the stone.*

86. Once used by a blacksmith, this "smithy box" now serves as a magazine or newspaper rack in the living room of a collector. The knife on the side is an IXL blade used for cleaning horses' hoofs prior to shoeing.

87. A prize in any collection is this fine old bull's-eye lantern. Many cows were milked or the chores done by the beam from such a lantern.

88. In the 1870s, the British invested heavily in the Santa Fe Railroad and the British Lion paperweights were sent over from England for use in the railroad depots. Hard to find now, they are interesting relics of the early-day railroads.

89. *The gold scales from the Wells Fargo, Columbia, California, office weighed some $50,000,000 worth of gold during their active career. Relics such as this are to be regarded as fabulous examples of Frontier Americana and the chances of a collector stumbling upon one are about 50,000,000 to one.*

smaller letters, is a unique lion paperweight. English investors plunked a right smart passel of sterling into our railroad ventures during the period when the iron hoss was supplanting the wagontrain. These paperweights were sent over to be used by station masters in the depots. The British Lion, made in England, an item of

Frontier Americana? You betcha! They're one thousand percent collectable as an accessory relating to early western railroading.

A chapter on the Wells Fargo office has been omitted

scales, *mochilas*, and original "Reward" posters are in the same category.

There are three small items, however, still around in limited quantity, which offer some opportunity for the

REWARD!

WELLS, FARGO & Co.'s EXPRESS BOX, on Chinese and Copperopolis Stage, was ROBBED this morning, by one man about two miles from Burns Ferry. (Ruplee's Bridge,) Tuolumne county side, of $600 in coin and gold dust.

For arrest and conviction of the Robber, we will pay $300, and one-fourth of any portion of treasure recovered.

ROBBER described as follows: A Mexican, lightish complexion, rather short and thick set; weight about 150 lbs.; had a moustache and short growth of beard.

JOHN J. VALENTINE,

San Francisco, Dec. 1, 1875.   TUOLUMNE INDEPENDENT PRINT.   General Superintendent.

90. Original "Reward" posters and public notices of Wells Fargo Express service are exceedingly scarce.

for two reasons.

First, the story of Wells Fargo has been the subject of so many books there is little that could have been related here without rehashing "twice-told" tales. Secondly, it's practically impossible to locate anything relating to Wells Fargo that isn't top-notch museum material and, consequently, way out of the ordinary collector's reach. The express box, for instance, is so classic an item it would take a king's ransom to secure one. Bank gold

collector to have the firm represented in his display cabinet. Wooden insulators, from early telegraph lines that paralleled the Pony Express routes, are vitally linked to the Wells Fargo saga. Some of these can still be found on rotted posts along the old trail. Sometimes stamp dealers are able to provide philatelic material—franked envelopes which were carried by riders and stagecoaches between terminal points along the route. Recently I found a money receipt issued by Wells Fargo among a lot

91. The wooden insulator shown here is an interesting fragment of Frontier Americana. It was found eighty miles south of Elko in an area where stumps of the old telegraph lines, which paralleled the Pony Express route across Nevada, remain.

of old correspondence in a deserted house. A few scraps of paper dealing with the Wells Fargo operation is about all one can hope to find these days.

The schoolhouse would have covered a lot of fascinating things that were incident to the "book larnin'" of the western kids: *McGuffey's Readers*, the teacher's brass bell, perhaps a dinner pail. I once found an orrery under an old tumbledown schoolhouse. Know what an orrery is? It's a mechanical apparatus with an arrangement of balls (earth, moon, sun, etc.) used to illustrate the move-

ments and phases of the planets in our solar system. They're sometimes called planetariums.

The accouterments of the military has been merely touched on in "At The Frontier Outpost." Mess gear, edged weapons, bullet molds, insignia, epaulets, cartridge boxes, pouches, etc. have valid claim to recognition.

And there's more. There's a wealth of broadsides, books, maps, territorial newspapers and periodicals, early mining and railroad stock certificates, wood engravings,

92. Wells Fargo money receipts, franked envelopes, advertising literature and similar paper items are about the only relics of the Express line still available to collectors.

93. Most noted of all early school books were McGuffey's New Eclectic Readers. Pictured here are the first three readers, together with an old school bell. Students often vied with each other to see who would ring the bell to begin school.

94. Dad used to buy cut plug in tin containers such as this, so the kids could use them for lunch pails.

lithographs, mezzotint engravings, and advertising literature which figured prominently in the lives and fortunes of Westerners.

WE'VE RIDDEN ALONG this trail together for quite a spell and there's a fork ahead where I have to turn off. You've still got a right smart piece to go and I shore wish I could ride along with you. I've heard tell of the shambles of an old stage station up that way and a ghost town a few miles off to the south, too. Not much left around there, I suppose, but it's important to recover and preserve whatever you may be fortunate enough to find.

These remnants of the Old West may be rusty and broken, weathered and worn, but each has a story to tell—a story of brave men and women and bold deeds. There's adventure and a rugged spirit that still clings to them; and, when you hold one of those relics in your hand you'll feel something inside. I can't explain it, but you've sensed it too, I'm sure. Maybe duty, country and honor is part of it.

Here's that fork in the trail, Podner, and regardless of what you find up the road—whether it be free as just stooping down and picking it up or whether it will belong to a steely-eyed gent you'll have to dicker with—here's hoping this little book will turn out to be the "equalizer" for you who are new at the game.

APPENDIX

READING ABOUT THE fascinating objects, gear, accessories and paraphernalia called "Frontier Americana" is one thing, but nothing quite compares to the exciting experience of finding your own relics. Since this is not always feasible, the next best thing is to view them in collections where they have been preserved. Listed here are a *few* representative displays located in our western states.

Arizona	Arizona State Museum, Tucson Trailside Museum, Tucson
California	Knott's Berry Farm and Ghost Town, Buena Park Wells Fargo Bank Museum, San Francisco
Colorado	Colorado State Museum, Denver Old Boca House and Pioneer Museum, Trinidad
Idaho	Pioneer Village, Boise State Historical Museum, Boise
Kansas	Old Abilene Town, Abilene Kansas State Historical Society and Museum, Topeka
Montana	Charles M. Russell Home, Great Falls Public Library Collection, Great Falls
	Thompson-Hickman Memorial Museum, Virginia City
Nebraska	State Historical Society and Museum, Lincoln Harold Warp Pioneer Village, Minden
Nevada	Old Mint Museum, Carson City State Historical Society, Carson City
New Mexico	Museum of New Mexico, Santa Fe
North Dakota	State Museum, Bismarck
Oklahoma	Woolaroc Museum, near Bartlesville National Cowboy Hall of Fame, Oklahoma City State Historical Building, Oklahoma City
Oregon	Grant County Museum, Canyon City
South Dakota	W. H. Over Museum, Vermillion
Texas	Amon Carter Museum of Western Art, Fort Worth Alamo Museum, San Antonio Pioneer Town, Wimberley
Utah	Pioneer Village, Salt Lake City Latter-Day Saints Museum, Salt Lake City

136

Washington   Washington State Museum, Seattle

Wyoming   Cody Museum, Cody

Western Americana Collection at
University of Wyoming Library,
Laramie

PICTURE CREDITS

1. *Scribner's Magazine*, March 1906. 2. Author's collection, photo by Robert Small. 3. Photo by Carrol Aston. 4. Sketch by the author. 5. Author's collection, photo by Carrol Aston. 6. From LANGFORD OF THE THREE BARS by Kate and Virgil D. Boyles. Published in Chicago, 1907, by A. C. McClurg and Company. 7. Author's collection, photo by Carrol Aston. 8. From LANGFORD OF THE THREE BARS. 9. Herschel C. Logan collection. 10. Herschel C. Logan collection. 11. Herschel C. Logan collection. 12. Betty Elliot collection. 13. Sketch by the author. 14. Sketch by the author. 15. Sketch by the author. 16. Author's collection, photo by Robert Small. 17. Author's collection, photo by Robert Small, and sketches by the author. 18. Sketch by the author. 19. Sketches by the author. 20. Author's collection, photo by Carrol Aston. 21. Author's collection, photo by Carrol Aston. 22. Sketch by the author. 23. Author's collection, photo by Carrol Aston. 24. Author's collection, photo by Carrol Aston. 25. From *Harper's Monthly Magazine*, September, 1888. 26. Norvell-Shapleigh Hardware Company catalog, 1903. 27. Betty Elliot collection. 28. Pat Wagner collection, photo by Carrol Aston. 29. Betty Elliot collection. 30. From the Wells Fargo Bank History Room, San Francisco, California. 31. *Frank Leslie's Popular Monthly*, July, 1903. 32. Herschel C. Logan collection. 33. From an 1862 history book, title and publisher unknown. 34. Hershel C. Logan collection. 35. Herschel C. Logan collection. 36. Herschel C. Logan collection. 37. Author's collection, photo by Robert Small. 38. Herschel C. Logan collection. 39. From "Laskar" by Hugh Johnson, *Scribner's Magazine*, August, 1907. 40. Herschel C. Logan collection. 41. Herschel C. Logan collection. 42. Herschel C. Logan collection. 43. Herschel C. Logan collection. 44. Herschel C. Logan collection.

45. Herschel C. Logan collection. 46. *Scribner's Magazine*, March 1906. 47. Author's collection, photo by Robert Small. 48. Herschel C. Logan collection. 49. Author's collection, photo by Robert Small. 50. Author's collection, photo by Robert Small. 51. Author's collection, photo by Robert Small. 52. Author's collection, photo by Robert Small. 53. Author's collection, photo by Robert Small. 54. Author's collection, photo by Robert Small. 55. *Harper's New Monthly Magazine*. 56. *Harper's New Monthly Magazine*. 57. Herschel C. Logan collection. 58. Herschel C. Logan collection. 59. Herschel C. Logan collection. 60. Author's collection, photo by Robert Small. 61. Herschel C. Logan collection. 62. Jug and Mag Wayman collection. 63. Author's collection, photo by Robert Small. 64. Herschel C. Logan collection. 65. *Scribner's Magazine*, March, 1906. 66. Author's collection, photo by Robert Small. 67. Herschel C. Logan collection. 68. Sketch by the author. 69. Author's collection, photo by Robert Small. 70. *Collier's Weekly*, January 26, 1901. 71. Author's collection, photo by Robert Small. 72. Herschel C. Logan collection. 73. *Harper's New Monthly Magazine*. 74. Author's collection, photo by Robert Small. 75. Author's collection, photo by Robert Small. 76. *Scribner's Magazine*, January, 1906. 77. From "A Day With the Round-Up," *Scribner's Magazine*, March, 1906. 78. *Scribner's Magazine*, October, 1907. 79. Author's collection. 80. From "A Day With the Round-Up," *Scribner's Magazine*, March, 1906. 81. Herschel C. Logan collection. 82. Sketch by author. 83. Photo courtesy Ralph A. Coffeen. 84. Photo courtesy Ralph A. Coffeen. 85. Herschel C. Logan collection. 86. Herschel C. Logan collection. 87. Herschel C. Logan collection. 88. Herschel C. Logan collection. 89. Photo courtesy Wells Fargo Bank History Room, San Francisco,

California. 90. Photo courtesy Wells Fargo Bank History Room, San Francisco, California. 91. Collection of Western Publications, Austin, Texas, photo by Robert Small. 92. Author's collection. 93. Herschel C. Logan collection. 94. Herschel C. Logan collection.